hWalls

The Rights of Memory

The Franklin Lectures in the Sciences and Humanities

AUBURN UNIVERSITY
Edited by Taylor Littleton

Volume 1:
Approaching the Benign Environment
Volume 2:
The Shape of Likelihood:
Relevance and the University
Volume 3:
Our Secular Cathedrals:
Change and Continuity in the University
Volume 4:
A Time to Hear and Answer:
Essays for the Bicentennial Season
Volume 5:
The Rights of Memory:
Essays on History, Science, and American Culture

The Franklin Lectures series finds
its principal purpose in addressing
the pervasive problem of people's
retaining their humanity and ideals within
a rapidly developing scientific and
technological society. Each volume
illuminates one element of the
critical relationship between cultural
tradition and scientific discovery and
accomplishment through the analyses
and perceptions of distinguished
figures from each of the "two cultures."

The
Rights
of
Memory

Essays on History, Science, and American Culture

THE FRANKLIN LECTURES IN THE
SCIENCES AND HUMANITIES
edited by TAYLOR LITTLETON

THE UNIVERSITY OF ALABAMA PRESS

"The American Scholar in the Twenty-first Century"
by Daniel J. Boorstin, Copyright © 1984 by Daniel J. Boorstin
"Modern Science and Contemporary Discomfort:
Metaphor and Reality" by Leon N Cooper,
Copyright © 1984 by Leon N Cooper
"History and Its Enemies: Writers and the Civil War"
by William S. McFeely,
Copyright © 1984 by William S. McFeely

Library of Congress Cataloging in Publication Data
Main entry under title:
The Rights of memory.

(The Franklin lectures in the sciences & humanities)
Bibliography:p.
Includes index.
1. United States—Intellectual life—Addresses,
essays, lectures. 2. United States—Civilization—Ad-
dresses, essays, lectures. 3. Science—Social aspects—
United States—Addresses, essays, lectures. 4. United
States—Historiography—Addresses, essays, lectures.
I. Littleton, Taylor. II. Series.
E169.1.R57 1986   973   85-13972
ISBN 0-8173-0278-6 (alk. paper)

I have some rights of memory in this kingdom,
Which now to claim my vantage doth invite me.

—Fortinbras to Horatio, *Hamlet* V, ii, 378–79

Contents

Suggestions for Further Reading

The Rights of Memory

Introduction

TAYLOR LITTLETON

The manufacturing of Procrustean beds is an art especially cultivated by those who write Introductions to collections of essays: a stretch here, a constriction there, and all eventually are uncomfortably tucked in. Such a procedure would seem particularly relevant as one approaches a group of essays delivered originally as lectures over a three-year period, with each writer essentially unaware of the content to be developed by the others. Indeed, such has consistently been a pattern during the fifteen-year history of the Franklin Lectures Series, whose purpose has been to enrich the cultural and academic life of Auburn University through discussions of interdisciplinary relationships between the "two cultures." Within this framework, Lecturers from both the sciences and the humanities have generally proceeded to identify and address topics broad in scope, yet indigenous to their own scholarly interests and concerns. In the present case, Daniel Boorstin *did* know that Jaroslav Pelikan would deliver a tribute to Emerson on the centenary of his death, and thus chose to project Emerson's "American Scholar" figure into the twenty-first century. Both William McFeely and James M. Cox proposed to sustain their scholarly interests in Grant and Civil War themes; Richard M. Brown and Leon Cooper each agreed to consider certain contemporary issues which appear to have, at least in part, nineteenth-century origins; and Elizabeth Fox-Genovese chose to develop an extended statement on our need to revise the story of the past which we have inherited from the "great tradition." Yet, though each essay was independently developed, they would appear to merge without violence into a balanced and coherent repose.

Each essay, including that by physicist Leon Cooper, projects a general theme of "history": its definition and its proper function within the culture. There are, of course, divergent views, but each seems to find in its opposite a response which enriches and clarifies the territory. To Boorstin, for example, the applications of technology are gradually eroding what he calls our "republic of letters," founded on a sense of shared knowledge and sustained through the "additive" scholarship of the humanities which continually enriches the past and illuminates the present. On the other hand, we now see gradually emerging a "republic of technology" based on shared experience consumed within a system of mass culture and augmented by the "cumulative" effort of the scientist which consistently replaces and makes obsolete past achievements through new discoveries. Cooper, however, sees the scientist, like the historian, as creating and continually modifying or reinterpreting metaphors of the past. To the scientist, such metaphors may function as images of reality as they are shown to agree with experience in the natural world; and while they may in fact displace views of the world which no longer contain such agreements, these images, based as they are on structure and demonstrable relationships, need not violate the authenticity of visions which must be created within the memory and imagination as historians also seek ways to explain and make whole our present condition and to send forward, as it were, messages of continuity to the future.

These themes of cultural confusion between metaphor and reality and the assumed insensitivity of science to the comprehensive past directly connect the essays of Boorstin and Cooper to Pelikan's discussion of Emerson's visionary fusion of the "two cultures." While Emerson's views about the promise and possibilities of science may indeed be a characteristic expression of the optimism and faith in progress of early nineteenth-century America, they gain originality and significance here through his sense of a revelatory connection, a humanistic coherence, between the scientific study of natural phenomena and the scholarly review of the lives of "great men." To Emerson, both "natural history" and "human history" separately illuminate the presence of order and design in the nature of things; and, together, they yield a unified sense of wholeness as the harmonious proportions of the natural world, including man's place in it, gradually revealed by the progressive and courageous investigations of the scientist, find a dynamic though mysterious parallel in the emergence of great men whose purpose is to break with tradition and the lifeless past.

Surely it is possible for us to sense across the years a certain affinity between Emerson's intuitive feeling for the harmony and proportion he read in the book of nature and Cooper's reassuring projection of science as a metaphor of order and structure. But, as Pelikan makes clear, Emerson saw no conflict between traditional religious values and the clarifications of the natural world being continually revealed by the discoveries of nineteenth-century science. Indeed, science seemed to him even a promising alternative to inherited theology. And though he serenely subordinated the mere utilitarian applications of science in favor of what was to him the deeper reality, it is of interest to note his early instinctive understanding that one practical way in which the American Scholar could break his traditional subservience to the older culture was by asserting himself toward superior achievements in science. Yet by the time of his death in 1882, Emerson's optimistic and elevated views of scientific investigation, as expressed in both *Nature* (1836) and *Representative Men* (1849), were being eroded, on the one hand, by the growth of a fundamentalist Protestantism, which increasingly viewed science as a threat to religious dogma, and on the other by an emerging apprehension about technology and its subordination of human values. Both Boorstin, in his expressed concern that technology tends to separate our contemporary life from its past, and Cooper, in his discussion of our modern discomfort with science, affirm and record the historical separation of the two cultures in American intellectual life.

But if the three essays by Pelikan, Boorstin, and Cooper together yield a perspective on the uneasy relationship in America between science and a sense of history, the further essays in the volume reveal certain affinities. In a sense, Cooper's desire to ameliorate our modern discomfort with science, so that it can be regarded "without terror," is akin to the proposals of William McFeely and Elizabeth Fox-Genovese to create an altered approach to the writing of history, so that its province and service to society can be properly determined. And it would be difficult to find an essay more illustrative than that by Richard M. Brown (on violence in American history) of several themes sounded by Boorstin, McFeely, and Fox-Genovese: the importance of recording into survival the episodes of daily life acted out by ordinary men and women; sustaining the "democracy" of historical writing by disclosing to one's fellow citizens how the past is directly relevant to their contemporary lives; and in the process illustrating an historical methodology which blends the analysis of traditional recorded materials of manuscript and public record with demographic modes of investigation.

But does the scholarship inherent in the diverse topics covered by these essays, composed as they were in innocent isolation from each other, unexpectedly set forth an organic and interconnected relationship which helps to define and illustrate the duty of the scholar: as Boorstin would say, a figure to serve as a courier of time, confirming messages to both present and future of continuity and relevance; or, as McFeely, to seek out the imaginative connections suggested in the historical memory; or, as Fox-Genovese, to examine anew the "official" stories of our culture and the "rights" of those who tell them; or, as Emerson, to see something of the whole in the part? Possibly not, at least on the grand and majestic scale whereby science visualizes a wondrous affinity between events from distant galaxies and the condition of living cells. Nevertheless, there are connections. For example, within the silent and noncommittal order of chronology itself two highly symbolic events, described respectively by Cox and Brown, converge: the huge reunion in Chicago of the Army of the Tennessee on November 13, 1879, at which General Grant was chief guest, and the bloody shoot-out on the following May 11th, many hundreds of miles away in the shining wheat fields surrounding Mussel Slough, California. It is no matter that the evening at the Palmer House is famous because of Mark Twain's speech on the occasion or that, as McFeely has observed in his biography of Grant, the event anticipated the end of Grant's third-term aspirations. Nor is it difficult to observe that the crackling gunfire and violent deaths of that hot California afternoon had somehow been informed by the policies of Grant's own presidential administration, which had stimulated the frontier land wars through enabling legislation, allowing powerful corporations, such as the Southern Pacific Railroad, literally to dispossess the pioneer settlers of Mussel Slough. What unexpectedly binds the two events together is that the veterans of Shiloh, Corinth, and Cold Harbor who restlessly endured those six hours of oratory were remembering one war of civil strife while another was taking shape—less spectacular, to be sure, but one whose pattern of violence still rends the social fabric of American life. This pattern, as Brown makes clear, has been deeply influenced by the migration of rural Americans to urban settings, bringing with them, in the process, not only a heightened propensity toward violence but also a heritage of the "homestead ethic," the right to own and defend a home of one's own. The conflict of this rural "homestead" heritage with current inflationary economic conditions in the metropolis threatens, particularly for the young, the remnant of the American dream of success. And as one reflects on this complex matrix of national values as set forth by Brown—their origin in the nineteenth-century frontier experience, their transportation and frustrating encounter with the economic closures of urban America—it is not difficult to sense its communion with another broad social theme appearing in this collection: the strange and vigorous resurrection of the "creationists" and their challenge of science and its prerogatives.

Our own post-war experience with the threats of environmental pollution and nuclear annihilation are genuine reasons for the hostile views toward science with which Cooper takes issue. But these widely projected apprehensions would seemingly have little to do with the creationist stance. In addition to the homestead ethic, the traditional religious values of rural Americans were also, of course, part of the nineteenth-century heritage conveyed to the city, to the centers of the republic of technology where residence became increasingly conditioned by the accelerating rate of change and, also, by an obsession for instant retrieval and wide dissemination of the topical. The subsequent bewilderment and historical disorientation—in Boorstin's phrase, a "chronological myopia"—together with, as Cooper observes, the gradual disappearance of nineteenth-century expectations that a value system would emerge from science itself to replace that eroded by the scientific world view, undoubtedly lie behind the reactionary retreat to a fundamentalist vision of reality. The rituals of indecision and frustration, manifest in the whole creationist issue; their absorption by a highly vocal portion of society, and their surprising influence on political and educational debate reveal a deep insecurity about the place and meaning of religion in the national consciousness of twentieth-century America.

Indeed, within the unconscious but binding array of relationships we are seeking within these essays, the strident, condemning, and passionate rhetoric with which the creationist sense of cultural dispossession is typically expressed finds a distant but illuminating counterpoint in the elegant and almost liturgical prose, quoted by Brown, of the appeal sent in 1880 to President Rutherford B. Hayes by hundreds of Mussel Slough settlers, asking that they be protected from the ravages of railroad dispossession and emphasizing their hard work in converting a wasteland into an American community of "peace and order, honesty, decency and plenty": to be sure, into a "garden."

And what further may be said of Grant himself, with whom this inquiry into linkages began? It is not likely, as the familiar Civil War place names from Tennessee, Mississippi, and Virginia converged in the smoky air during that long and noisy evening at the Palmer House, that Grant had already begun to project himself autobiographically and thus resolve the contradictions of his life and career. Yet within the half-decade initiated by the Chicago reunion and the Mussel Slough gunfight, his political and personal fortunes, together with his health, declined; his response was the *Personal Memoirs*. Grant was not a "great man" in Emerson's sense of the term, but he was surely, like Emerson, a "representative man" of his century. Emerson himself died (as did Darwin) during this same half-decade, within which composition of the *Memoirs* literally completed Grant's life. The radical and nontraditional thought which marked Emerson's early career as essayist and lecturer is now but a nostalgic element in the national memory of an America which has long since outgrown its optimistic and "dangerous" origins. And perhaps we now remember even less clearly his later return, in the midst of the war itself, to some of these themes; to him, the war had thrown into strong relief the perilous condition of American democracy, the nation's arrogance, its passion for materialism and blindness to human rights, the failure of the scholar-intellectual to participate in the life of his times. During the very year in which Grant assumed command of the Union army, Emerson was vigorously proclaiming his message throughout New England, and would in the next two years exhort thousands more in the most active lecture tour of his career.*

While something deep in the conscience of many Americans was listening to Emerson and helping to define for us his ethical image, Grant's connection with the national experience, if no more pervasive than Emerson's, was by 1864 beginning to assume its more pragmatic and evident form. His ambition; his commercial motive in undertaking the *Memoirs;* his belief set forth therein that his rise to fame from unpromising beginnings was somehow illustrative of the unexpected possibilities inherent in democracy; his casual though truly astonishing observation, illuminating (as it does) national patterns of American behavior: that in the field, one is driven toward destruction of the enemy because of the lack of moral courage to retreat; his financial failures and his presidential ineptness—all of these seem less important than the life that was

---

*In 1865 alone, Emerson, much in demand, delivered seventy-seven lectures in the North and West. Cf. Gay Wilson Allen, *Waldo Emerson* (New York: Viking, 1981), pp. 620ff.

crystallized and assumed its larger relevance during the few years of the war primarily described in the *Memoirs*. That life, as Cox's essay makes clear, possessed the qualities of the prose style that described it in the *Memoirs* and that first appeared in Grant's battle orders during the war: clarity, plainness, restraint, and an organic sense of purpose which drives the narrative of the *Memoirs* relentlessly forward, as if in pursuit of the enemy itself. As any military historian can tell us, Grant, too, superseded tradition, recognizing instinctively and with great foresight the changing dynamics of warfare and its comprehensive nature, as few had before him. Nondescript but implacable, he integrated the scattered elements and elliptical energy of the Army of the Republic toward its chilling objective of totally destroying the enemy. Within this confined but crucial parameter of the war, Grant became, perhaps, the first of the "new men" who would follow him in the second half of the century, generals of commerce like Leland Stanford, Rockefeller, and Carnegie, who would help to shape the developing nation by discerning, organizing, and bringing under control its vast though latent industrial power, dispossessing their opposition in no less relentless and single-minded a manner than Grant had exhibited in the field.

Here, then, are strange configurations indeed: the homestead ethic and the myth of Genesis, Shiloh and Mussel Slough, Unconditional Surrender Grant and the Sage of Concord; and, too, lying amidst this authenticated history are those latent interconnections silently waiting to emerge, symbolized perhaps, in Fox-Genovese's description, by the funeral scene of a woman who had witnessed and transmitted orally to her grand-daughter a vision of the unrecorded past but whose life was mourned by the words and sounds of our officially remembered values. But however imperfectly perceived and discussed here, the very presence of such relationships illustrates at least part of the message of these randomly composed essays: that there are patterns, structures in the past, connections which can legitimately emerge in unexpected forms through the scholarly fusion of what McFeely calls "memory and imagination." Science, as it continually discovers new elements in the reality of how the world works, must necessarily displace presumptuous metaphors of reality which cannot be tested by experience, perhaps revealing in the process deep-seated uncertainties and frustrations within the social order as our assumed rights of memory seem dispossessed. Boorstin reminds us that the scholar of the future must carry the burden of recording both the metaphors and the realities—and one might say the frustrations as well—in the shaping of the human tale. The emphasis on the immediate within the republic of technology may indeed be a deterrent to recording and retaining the wholeness of the past. But it would seem that even more formidable is the sense of infinitude of time and space initiated in the nineteenth century by Darwinism and augmented by the new physics of the twentieth, an imagery of vastness against which men and women, their accomplishments and reputations, ebb and flow into forgetfulness.

The laser of continuity necessary to penetrate this modern vision of human life must be acts of scholarship which beam through time quiet but insistent messages of the significance within the lives of both representative and ordinary men. The scholar must be not only a courier, but a sentinel of time: for wholeness and for the polyforms of meaning which continually coalesce and disappear, thereby assisting the culture to distinguish between the rich artifacts of history and its sustained reemerging truths. And if this broadly communicative scholarship is not written in McFeely's "language used in diners," with Grant's plainness, or in the aggressive economic style of converse among workmen overheard by Emerson in Boston's North End, it should at least be expressed in language sufficiently democratic to be useful in such promising and practical efforts as the publicly supported programs which are beginning to bring scholars into local communities to stimulate interactive discussions on topics of continuing humanistic concern. Linking the messages of scholarship to the individual life, of course, has ever been a problem: to reduce, in Cooper's figure, the absurdity of the play that many individual citizens choose merely to watch, rather than engage, because they feel separated from any background of moral and ethical belief to guide them into meaningful social action.

In this connection, some of the present essayists recall the remarks of Robert Penn Warren, made earlier in this series, that only through the discipline of studying the past can the self gain a sense of identity and a fulfilling relationship with others: indeed, it is only by earning a place in the general human story that one can affect the creation of the future. The act of will necessary for the scholar-messenger of the twenty-first century to make his lonely and self-appointed rounds is undoubtedly still latent in our universities, libraries, and research centers, for his mission and burden would seem to be but ethical translations of the lingering and persistent desire of each of us to be not merely witnesses of the story but to be participants in it—and to have that participation somehow understood.

To be sure, the present essays directly or by implication stress America's dilemma with its own history, a dilemma complicated by conditions in the republic of technology. Yet it is encouraging to find permanently recorded in the wider life of the culture those central themes of engagement and continuity with which the scholarship described and demonstrated herein is concerned. Warren's very words, for example, are prefigured in those of Shakespeare's Enobarbus, who, on the vast historical stage encompassing both Rome and Egypt, had been essentially a witness of the action, an impersonal commentator on the behavior of "great men"; but by his moral decision to enter the tragic pattern of Antony's career, he defines his own identity and, as he says, "earns a place in the story," a place which all his clever observation and opulent description of Cleopatra's barge could never create. And finally, what distant voice from our imaginative history could speak to us more clearly than that of Shakespeare's most "representative man"? Hamlet's is the quintessential message to the future from the individual life and from our century, for it is "to tell my story," to "report . . . my cause aright" that with his dying words he commissions Horatio. No one more than he has felt the burdens of the past; and, like most of us, he too had been a witness, inhibited from full participation in the unfolding sequence of experience by its perplexing and seemingly contradictory nature.

But Hamlet, like Enobarbus, creates the future by the moral act of engaging the past, of entering and thereby earning not only his place in the story but earning as well the right to have it told to the "yet unknowing world." Will that story with its explanation of the past ("How these things came about") help to sustain the realm? And will our own messages, as we seek to transcend our time and our place, even be received? The unlikely figure of Fortinbras, to whom Hamlet's story is offered, might serve as an image of the future awaiting our own time. Warlike, inscrutable, he yet aligns himself with that story: "I have some rights of memory in this kingdom," and his response to the message of the past beams reassuringly down the centuries:

Let us haste to hear it,
And call the noblest to the audience.

The American Scholar in the Twenty-first Century

DANIEL J. BOORSTIN

I have chosen as my theme "The American Scholar in the Twenty-first Century," and I must first suggest what I mean by the American Scholar and also what I do not mean. I exclude from my definition and my special concern this afternoon the natural or physical or medical scientist. For my purpose and for our exploration together, everybody else is a scholar. "The scholar," then, includes all those whom we would describe as humanists or social scientists.

I know that in later lectures in this series, my admired friend, Professor Jaroslav Pelikan, will be here—and I will urge all of you to come to hear his lectures—he is one of the most brilliant and perceptive lecturers and one of the most cosmopolitan scholars I have ever known. I know he is looking forward to coming and we have talked about his theme, the ideas of Ralph Waldo Emerson, whom I find to be not one of the most lively of scholars, but I am sure you will find that Professor Pelikan will make him so. In 1837, in his "American Scholar," which is probably the most famous utterance under that title that has ever been made in this country, Emerson made a statement which has come to be known as our intellectual declaration of independence. Emerson, you may recall, said, "Our day of dependence, our long apprenticeship to the learning of other lands, draws to a close. We have listened," he said, "too long to the courtly muses of yore." I will dare to pursue Emerson's purpose—that is to discover the role and mission of thinkers in our society now and in the future, but like Emerson I am especially concerned with those of our thinkers who dealt primarily not with the mastery of nature but with the world of man and of society. I will show, I hope, how these are connected and how our ways of mastering nature shape the role of our scholars. Emerson was concerned that Americans would not be immersed totally enough in the special experience of their time and place—in a word, that they would not be American enough. I have another concern and another theme. I would like to think that I, too, am trying to utter a declaration of independence, but mine aims to be a declaration of independence of our time.

I have chosen the title "The American Scholar in the Twenty-first Century," not because I will claim clairvoyance, but because I want to emphasize the role of the American scholar which is required by the direction and momentum of American life in our time, a momentum which is likely to increase, to accelerate, to become increasingly dominant in the decades to come. Despite the complexity of all these forces which converge on us, my theme, as you will see, is quite simple. But I must begin by reminding you that the role of the scholar, the role of anyone who would lift us out of our time, is always difficult. It is difficult because of what I would call the bias of survival. The bias of survival is a name for the difficulties of reaching back into the past and seeing the way things really were. There is no better introduction to this problem than a parable which is told by that wonderfully versatile atomic scientist, Leo Szilard, in his work "The Voice of the Dolphins," which I hope you will all read. The parable which he tells is in the form of what he calls a report on Grand Central Terminal. It was prepared—will have been prepared, perhaps—by explorers from another planet who arrive at the site of what used to be New York City before an atomic holocaust totally destroyed the city. After they have investigated the site, they report that they have learned some interesting things about this extinct civilization, and I will mention only three of the things that they discover.

First, they discover that the railroad cars stored in the station were labeled either smokers or nonsmokers—clearly, they say, indicating some sort of segregation of passengers. There may have lived in the city, they say, two strains of earth dwellers—a more pigmented variety, having a dark or smoky complexion, and a less pigmented variety, though not necessarily albino, they say, having a fair or nonsmoky complexion.

After visiting the remains nearby of what was an art museum, they widen their understanding of those extinct earthlings. A certain percentage of the images on the canvas in the frames disclose the existence of a third strain of earth dwellers. This strain has, in addition, they say, to a pair of hands and legs, a pair of wings, and apparently all of them belong to the less pigmented variety; none of the numerous skeletons, however, so far exhumed seem to have belonged to the winged strain. They propose that we have to deal here with the images of an extinct variety. And this hypothesis is confirmed by the fact which they notice: that the winged forms are much more frequently found among the older paintings than among the more recent paintings.

Their third, and in some ways their most interesting discovery, came when they found two small halls located in a rather hidden position. Each of these halls, labeled "men" or "women," contained a number of small cubicles. The door of each and every cubicle was locked by a rather complicated gadget. Upon investigation of these gadgets, it was found that they contained a number of round metal discs. These ingenious gadgets barred entrance to the cubicle until an additional disc was introduced into them through a slot. All the discs had in common the word "liberty" inscribed on them. They concluded that it designated a virtue held in high esteem and to which the extinct earth dwellers made a sacrifice of the disc when they entered the cubicle. They also noted that these cubicles were not found in a single one of the small lodging houses, and so they concluded that the ceremonial act in worship of the virtue liberty was performed only in public places.

Now the difficulties which the visitors to this planet in the next century may have, in the unhappy event of a holocaust of that kind, are difficulties which I have experienced myself, in my own historical research, in a slightly different way. And I will suggest to you some of the problems which I have encountered.

In trying to find out what people read in the colonial period, especially in the field of religion, I discovered that their most widely reported school texts—in the form of hornbooks or the *New England Primer*—were among the most difficult to discover. An original hornbook from the seventeenth century is very hard to find and, although we have some *New England Primers* from the eighteenth century, the seventeenth-century versions are practically impossible to come upon. By contrast, if I wanted to consult the heavy theological treatises, the writings of Thomas Shepard or the Mathers, I found these sets in the rare book rooms of many great libraries, sometimes with uncut pages.

I found similarly when I came down to the nineteenth century and wanted to discover what people thought of their great men, that among the most commonly reproduced pieces of printed matter were the so-called Crockett almanacs which were printed—some of them not so far from here—in 30,000 or 40,000 copies. They were, or course, handed about, carried in saddle bags, passed around in bars and at campfires and worn thin. They were very difficult to find and very costly if you could come upon them. By contrast, if you are interested in finding a set of John Marshall's five-volume life of George Washington—which was one of the publishing disasters of the nineteenth century—you can find sets of it in numerous second-hand furniture stores.

This led me to a hypothesis which explains some of the difficulties of us historians. I call it the "law of the survival of the unread." This is only one of the problems that I have encountered in trying to discover what people really read and what they really thought. Another is a tendency toward the survival of the official and the proprietary. When Ruth and I visited the National Library in Budapest a few years ago, we were shown 120,000 proprietary charters certifying who owned certain pieces of land and what rights they had. These were the official documents, but there was no record of the human experience of the people who had those pieces of property. Because these documents were official and proprietary, they were preserved, but the details of the daily lives went unchronicled.

Similarly, there is a tendency toward the survival of the academic and the respectable. You might generalize this by saying that theology outlives pornography. The curricular outlives the extracurricular. Then there is the survival of the controversial, which tends to obscure the currents of daily life. What passes for the history of religion in courses in American civilization is really the history of religious controversy. We learn about the debates over the fine points in the theology of Jonathan Edwards, about the Americanist controversy in the Catholic Church and elsewhere. But what was religion then, in the daily lives of Americans, as expressed in their grace at table, in the daily prayers by the bedside? These currents of everyday life were not often recorded. What was not controversial was most intimate and most vivid to living people. But it was seldom recorded, and has not much interested historians.

Similarly, I have been trying for many years to learn something about the history of American food habits. And if you want to discover exactly what was eaten by a working class or middle class family in the eighteenth or nineteenth century, it is very difficult. But if you want to read the history of controversies over food, you will discover a considerable literature on vegetarianism, or on the prohibition movement, and on all the other controversies about what people should— and especially what they should not—eat. We encounter a similar difficulty when we try to chronicle the history of the family. There have been a number of efforts to write the history of the family in the United States, none of them quite successful. There is really, I would say, no good comprehensive history of the family in American life. On the other hand, we do have some excellent histories of divorce—which is a much easier subject to chronicle. There is a natural tendency, then, toward the survival of the controversial, but in most of our lives the daily currents go unchronicled.

There is another bias, which I would call the bias of success, which affects the record we have before us for all of our past experience. In the history of the American Revolution we all know that the history of the revolutionaries is very well reported but that, by comparison, there has been only a meager history of the loyalists. The loyalists were the losers; the revolutionaries were the winners. Similarly, in the history of the American Civil War, there is a tendency to treat American history generally as the history of unionism. But we know that when the Puritans came to this country from England, they did not come to build a stronger British Empire. When Americans moved westward across the continent, they moved to secede from a society which they felt was beginning to be decadent and they went in search of opportunity. The history of the United States could just as well be written as the history of secessionism, instead of the history of unionism. But it seems that because unionism won, that theme dominates our history.

In the history of technology, similarly, we read a story of successes. We hear glib talk of the firsts—for example, of Henry Ford's success in building an internal combustion engine. But how many people there were who were struggling to make such an engine who did not succeed and whom, therefore, we do not list among the American heroes! Some of those difficulties, of course, are chronicled in the bank accounts of lawyers, who tend to profit from the controversies over firsts and successes. One of the most profitable litigations in American history was that between George Selden and Henry Ford as to which one of them had succeeded as the first inventor of a gasoline-driven car. The people who really succeeded were the lawyers. But perhaps the most interesting and certainly one of the most useful parts of the history of technology is the history of the unsung heroes—of those who tried and didn't quite make it.

Finally, there is a tendency toward the survival of the durable. This, I suspect, is one of the reasons why we overemphasize the role of religion in past civilizations—because the places of death, the tombs, the pyramids, and the religious monuments, the cathedrals and the churches, and the sacred books tend to survive while other aspects of life tend to be dissolved and leave only ephemeral records. The emphasis on the monumental is often misleading. When we think of classical Greece, we think of the chaste white marble (now turned cream) of the Parthenon and the other buildings on the Acropolis. We forget that if we had seen the Acropolis in the great age of Greece, it would have looked much more like the grounds of an American World's Fair. Those buildings were garishly painted, but the colors disappeared and we are left with our textbook concept of "classical" architecture.

Of course, these are difficulties that have always afflicted the historian—but the role of the historian in the future will be even more difficult in his effort to establish our community with a whole past, to recapture the whole of human experience. One of the reasons for this is the movement from what was called the Republic of Letters to the Republic of Technology. I would like briefly to describe this transformation, how it came about, and what its consequences may be.

In the seventeenth and eighteenth centuries, men of culture frequently referred to what they called "the Republic of Letters." And the Republic of Letters was the community of people who were held together by a common devotion to and a common sharing of what they found in books. This republic was held together by shared knowledge—by a sharing of, an understanding and a reaching for, what was in the past. Now in our time, we have seen, especially since the Industrial Revolution, less and less emphasis on shared knowledge and a greater emphasis on shared experience. This emphasis has been made possible by the consumption and use of similar objects, by the perfecting of communication resulting in increasingly shared experience. The older Republic of Letters applied the test of time. Two centuries ago, George Crabbe called libraries "the tombs of such as cannot die." Or, in Ezra Pound's familiar phrase, literature is "news that stays news." The great works were immortal—they accumulated, they became monuments, they enriched one another. They survived the test of time.

But the Republic of Technology gives us another set of recognitions, and is committed to a wholly different set of preferences. This is what I would call the test of space. A celebrity, the prototypical pseudo-hero of the Republic of Technology, is well known not through time, not from generation to generation, but through space. He or she is known *everywhere* for a brief period, and that everywhere is made possible, of course, by our electronic technology.

Where does this leave the librarian and the scholar—those who were brought up with and who inherit another set of dimensions, the dimensions of the Republic of Letters?—those who have been trained not to look about at what everybody values today, but who look back through time to see what has been valued and what remains valuable? Before I go further into the general consequences for the accessibility of the past, I would like to remind you of how this shift in perspective has produced a kind of bewilderment, a kind of disorientation, among today's scholars.

There have been varied reactions to this change in orientation from the test of time to the test of space but I will mention only a couple of them—the temptations and difficulties that people in the world of letters encounter. First, there is a tendency, a temptation, to abandon the world of letters and to become an academic publicist or an academic demagogue, to appeal to the majority or the most vocal or most violent minorities of those living in the neighborhood. The resources for such appeals are richer than ever. There is another temptation or danger, to become peevish or irritable—to try to show that one thinks better than others by thinking the worst of others, especially of all the majority, past and present—which I would call the reaction of the knee-jerk anti-establishmentarian. The anti-establishmentarian attacks the present without using the arsenal of the past.

In our present situation, then, there is a special need for the scholar, as a special kind of messenger, explorer, prodder, remembrancer, in a world obsessed by the gospel of space—getting everything out to everywhere and in from everywhere instantly. We must try to be apostles of another gospel, the gospel of time, and make an effort to establish our community with the whole human past.

This role has become more difficult because of what I would call the contagion of science, the contagion of modern science and of scientific attitudes and institutions. All the institutions, the technologies and the opportunities that have led to the explosive development of science in this century have had the effect of increasing our orientation toward the present and the recent and making it more difficult for us to reach into the past. Until about the sixteenth or seventeenth century in Europe there was not so much difference between scientists, as we would call them, and other scholars. Both were almost equally oriented toward the past. The best, most respected knowledge had the patina of antiquity—whether it was in the world of humanities, of natural philosophy or even of technology. In those days before the rise of modern science, geographers and astronomers had their Ptolemy, physicians had their Galen, botanists had their Dioscorides, and everybody had his Aristotle. With the rise of the printing press and the professional author, of course, all traditional learning in every subject, including theology, came to be diluted by a larger admixture of recent and present publications. It was easier to add to the literature that people would read. Even humanists dared produce new classics and they even invented new genres like the novel. And, of course, new audiences arose—women and others who never read before—to invite and to be customers for this literature. And some would say this was to make literature more trivial than it had been. But the special character of modern science as it grew in the West was that science was more and more present-oriented and present-dominated than other realms of scholarship. The rise of the Royal Society in London, for example, and its counterparts across Europe at the end of the seventeenth and during the eighteenth century and the American Philosophical Society on this side of the Atlantic, made it possible for current trivia to become part of the stream of science. If you were a Leeuwenhoek in the Netherlands and looked through your magnifying glass and saw curious little creatures, you would send in word about that to the Royal Society in London— not in Latin—it didn't need to be in Latin. You could write in Dutch, in your vernacular, and that would be added to what came to be called science.

The transactions of the Royal Society and other similar publications brought science up to date. Now scientific celebrities—and sometimes we forget how many of the great figures of science were celebrities and not just heroes—celebrities like Sir Isaac Newton ruled the roost and arbitrated among those who claimed to be offering something new. Newton himself proudly and maliciously claimed his victory over Leibniz, in the invention of the calculus. Priority was the prize. The rise of modern science, then, is the rise of respect, awe, and appetite for the latest thing in facts and in theories. We forget that the word "scientist" did not come into our English language until about 1840. Luckily for us today, the non-scientist scholars remained oldfashioned in the literal sense of the word. For them the claim to attention came not from novelty but from durability, viability; no work could become a classic without the passage of time.

In science, by contrast, the important work is what we now call a breakthrough. We emphasize the melodramatic, explosive character of what has happened. The increasing dominance of science in our lives, the increasing pace of change of technology, put a greater and greater premium on novelty, which, of course, means the latest and the newest that stands in the foreground of time. While the scientist must be increasingly present-oriented, he depends less and less on books. He doesn't have time to wait for the printing press. He learns more and more through loose-leaf services, preprints, computer exchanges, or telephone calls. The scholar, however, still remains oriented to the whole past and especially, of course, to the book.

The multiplying new ways of exchanging information in science and technology have an effect, a by-product in attitudes toward the ancient stock of literature, humanistic knowledge, history and philosophy. One of the great problems we have in the Library of Congress, of course, is the simple quantity of matter, the number of items which come into the Library which we estimate now to be one and a half items every second of the working year. We keep large numbers of these items: we have estimated that we keep about 20 million books, but about 80 million items in other forms altogether—and our prime problem of selection and preservation really comes from the difference between our attitude and that of the modern scientist. If you will, contrast for a moment the kind of library that would best serve a modern physicist or chemist or other natural scientist with what would best serve all those whom I call the American scholars. It is crucial for a modern researcher in genetics to have the latest works and reports by his fellow scientists everywhere so that he can avoid repeating their mistakes and can build on their discoveries. A library of the latest works, the confirmed works, could be relatively small, but it must be kept up to date and kept current. Our problem at the Library of Congress, what makes our task enormous, and sometimes apparently unwieldy, is that we are a library of civilization, not just of science, not just of the latest thing, but of human history. We are as much interested in the missteps of other times and places as we are in their advances. We must have as complete a record as we can find of the rise of Nazism and of Adolf Hitler and his gang, and how the German people joined them, however false their work may have been to the advance of culture and civilization. But are the racial doctrines of Rosenberg and Streicher and the botanical dogmas of Lysenko of any value to the modern genetics library? The scientist is interested in the best and the latest product, but we scholars, students of the whole past, are interested in the spectrum—the complete extent of civilization and anti-civilization.

The role of the American scholar as mediator between past and present becomes more difficult because of what I call the contagion of science in the institutions of science and technology. And I will now remind you of some of the attitudes which predominate in the community of science. I do not disparage scientists for them; I simply describe them. These are attitudes which must be sharply contrasted with the attitudes of those whom I call the American scholars, but that contrast is something we sometimes overlook. I have already mentioned, of course, that the scientist and technologist must be present-oriented. This orientation, of course, is obvious—it's the most general distinction between the scientist and the scholar who must be interested in the whole of our past.

The scientist, moreover, is collaborative and, in our time, organization-oriented and interdependent. It is interesting to note how many Nobel Prizes are given not to one scientist, but to a pair or more. The Royal Society and its counterparts, the research and development laboratories of our time—which, by the way, have grown more than our universities since World War II—are a vivid contrast to the work of the writer. The writer, the scholar, is an individual—unique in his studio or in his library or at his typewriter or his word-processor. He must not wait to see what a colleague in Germany, in Britain, or elsewhere has lately discovered. But if you will read—I am sure some of you have read—James Watson's *Double Helix*, you will remember that among the most important guides to their activity in the calendar of their work in discovering the structure of the double helix was the news they constantly had and eagerly sought of what other scholars were doing. In one of the more disgusting passages in the modern literature of science, Watson unashamedly recounts the delight with which they toasted the failures of their colleagues on the other side of the Atlantic. The scientist is collaborative, organization-oriented and interdependent, but the scholar must be an often lonely but always idiosyncratic, courageous individual.

The technologist's goal, then, may be predictable—for example, he may go seeking the filament for the incandescent light bulb as Edison and his colleagues did, or the next generation of computers, which seems to be a next stage in a progression that is apparent. The scientist's work may be either predictable or startling. Whether in the accidental discovery of penicillin or in the concerted discovery that the atom is breakable, the breakthrough is the characteristic trait in the development of science. But the great scholar's work is neither predictable nor startling. And this is one of the problems in the effort to popularize humanistic scholarship. Humanists and those raising money to support their universities are tempted to claim the kudos of scientific breakthroughs. We should be wary of the claim that any new work of history is startling and shocking— that it is a "breakthrough." Humanistic works seldom are and need not be.

Of course, perhaps most obvious, the scientist lives in a world of quantification. The rise of science is another name for the increasing application of mathematics to the natural world, but the decline of historiography may perhaps be chronicled by the increasing application of quantification to human events. The scholar's world is a world of qualities—the kind of thing that the scientists think they have transcended. The scientist's world also is additive—each adds on to the previous view. In fact, the history of atomic physics is the series of steps in which each one advances beyond his predecessor—Szilard and Fermi, and so it goes. The next piece is to fill an empty space in the puzzle which seems clear from what has gone before. The scholar's work, however, is not quite that way; it is cumulative and transformative. The older becomes enriched by the later and is not obsoleted. Chaucer is enriched by Shakespeare, as T. S. Eliot has illustrated in his beautiful essay "Tradition and the Individual Talent," but Copernicus is not really much enriched by Einstein.

The scientist's pace of change is accelerated, increasing the momentum, increasing the rate of change—but not the scholar's. We will long recall the lament of John Adams when he contrasted the pace of science with that of political science. While the natural sciences had progressed remarkably in his own time, political science, he picturesquely observed, had not advanced much beyond what it was "at the time of the neighing of the horse of Darius." The world of science and technology can be transformed in a lifetime and has been transformed in our lifetime and is likely to be transformed in the future—perhaps in half-lifetimes. This means, of course, that the biology, chemistry, and physics textbooks I studied in school are obsolete, but not the books of literature.

The scientist and the technologist, moreover, must emphasize, and we are all grateful to them because they do emphasize, research and application. They are always asking what good can come of it. They, therefore, take a more solemn view of the world than the scholar does or should. For the scholar's emphasis is on delight and on enlightenment. What application has Shakespeare or Immanuel Kant? We must be willing to make applications. When we come to television, we encounter the ironic fact that many of our solemn academic friends object to television primarily because it is so full of entertainment—as if there were something particularly reprehensible in entertainment. In a scientifically oriented age all academics are tempted to think that whatever we learn must be uplifting and must have some application. But the difficult problem, of course, which many of us are working on, is how to encourage the development of those television programs which would not give entertainment a bad name. Of course, we can learn from the scientist. But I am urging this afternoon that we must insist on the special character of that view of the world which declares that the whole past is our treasure. The danger is one of contagion and imitation and enticement and even corruption by trying to get in on the rewards—the foundation grants, the money, the prestige and celebrity—that science properly earns in our time.

What, then, in summary, is the mission of the American scholar in the twenty-first century? I have suggested a convergence of forces. To the normal difficulty, the universal ancient difficulty of discovering the past because of what I call the bias of survival, modern science has added the bias toward the present and modern technology has immersed everyone in the trivia of the present. These new biases can drown us in the present. American scholars, then, all those who are not scientists, have a special urgent new mission. We are stationed on the borders between the past and the present. It is our task to expedite and communicate and to move, to help correct the chronological myopia of our time. Some of the messages that we might help our age learn might seem obvious or even cliché. We have a cautionary role; we can remind our time that every crisis is not Armageddon, that a headline is not an earthquake—which makes us anti-alarmists, of course, and anti-utopian. We can remind our time that every best-seller is not a classic. We must help sift the products of the past and the present and test the present by the past, and vice versa. We must keep open the channels and find our borders to the whole past, not just the fashionable or the newsworthy past. We must remind ourselves and all of our academic and other fellows of the perils of academic and journalistic ruts so that we can make an effort to get out of them.

We men and women of letters, then, the scholars of our century, the twenty-first century, are experimenters with time, seeking ways to cross the centuries as electronic scientists find ways to cross the continents, the oceans and outer space. We are keepers of the laboratory of preservation and perpetuation, seeking, and we hope, finding new ways of applying the test of time. If we can do this, we will enlarge the world of the present with full and wonderful and old chronological dimensions and bring urgent messages. First, the message of the similar, the message of continuity, that the present is no island, so we will not luxuriate in the pride of a false modernity. Then we may bring the message of the otherwise, so we will not luxuriate in the pride of a false necessity. We must, and can, serve our time by finding new ways to use the electronic present to advertise and stir the non-electronic past, to use the resources of the Republic of Letters to make us fuller, more active citizens of the republic, which now becomes a democracy of letters. We are the new couriers from past to present in an age when couriers through space seem to have become obsolete or at least obsolescent.

We tend to forget that it was Herodotus admiring the Persian couriers who first gave us a phrase that once was popular and even made good sense in another connection. He said the Persian messengers "travel

with a velocity which nothing human can equal; neither snow nor rain nor heat nor darkness are permitted
to obstruct their speed." This phrase is, of course, more
familiar in a slightly emended form in which it was
optimistically inscribed over the main United States
Post Office in New York City. Now I'm afraid it has a
sour and slightly ironic sound. But we may emend it
still to describe our mission and that of the American
scholar in the twenty-first century as the couriers of
time, and say that neither radio nor television nor computer nor gloom of newspapers nor charm of novelty
can stay us, the couriers of time, from the slow, never-
completed pursuit of our self-appointed rounds—messengers to the present from the past, messengers to our
time and place from all others.

Natural History Married to Human History: Ralph Waldo Emerson and the "Two Cultures"

JAROSLAV PELIKAN

The Franklin Lectures in the Sciences and Humanities are devoted to an examination of the relations between what the late C. P. Snow (himself an incumbent of the Franklin Lectureship) identified as "the two cultures" of the humanities and the natural sciences, or, to use an older term, "natural history" and "human history." In the history of the relations between the two, particularly within American thought, Ralph Waldo Emerson occupies a special place. And since April 27, 1982, is the centenary of Emerson's death, I propose, in these two Franklin Lectures, to examine the theme "Ralph Waldo Emerson and the 'Two Cultures.'"[1]

Emerson himself provided an appropriate title for such an examination, and in fact did so several times. In his *Journal* for August 15, 1834 (*JMN* 4:311), he observed: "Natural history by itself has no value; it is like a single sex. But marry it to human history, & it is poetry." When he first used the idea in public, just over a year later, on November 5, 1835, introducing his Boston lecture series on English Literature (*EL* 1:221), he had revised it to read: "All the facts in Natural History taken by themselves have no value, but are barren and unfruitful like a single sex. But marry it to human history and it is full of life." The same words, with "unfruitful" deleted, appeared in the first of his two lectures in that series on "Shakspear" [*sic*], delivered on December 10, 1835 (*EL* 1:289), and then became permanent by being incorporated into the fourth chapter of his first book, *Nature*, published in 1836 (*W* 1:28). (We shall be returning to that book in a moment.) Three times out of four, then, he stated that natural history, when married to human history, would be "full of life." But for the rest of his life, by deed and word (which are the same for Emerson, at least most of the time), he was proving that when his kind of "natural history" was married to his kind of "human history," the offspring truly would be his kind of "poetry"; and therefore I prefer the original version. In this first lecture I shall deal with "The Uses of Natural History," leading up to the publication of *Nature* in 1836, and with the reasons that he came to the conclusion, "Natural history by itself has no value." In the second lecture I shall go on to "The Uses of Great Men," leading to the publication of his *Representative Men* on January 1, 1850, and to the way his study of biography represented a marriage between natural history and human history—and therefore "poetry."

I. The Uses of Natural History

On November 6, 1833 (*L* 1:397), Charles Emerson wrote to his brother William Emerson: "Last evening

Waldo lectured before the Nat. Hist. Soc. to a charm. The young & the old opened their eyes & their ears—I was glad to have some of the stump lecturers see what was what & bow to the rising sun." A month before, and just a few days after his return from Europe, Waldo had written to William (*L* 1:397): "I have engaged to deliver the introductory Lecture to the Natural History Society in November." That lecture was given on November 5, 1833, under the title "The Uses of Natural History." It was the first of what was to be an uncounted number of public lectures that he would deliver over a period of nearly half a century. Coming as it did, almost precisely one year after his resignation from the pastorate of Second Church in Boston on October 28, 1832, the lecture of November 5 and those that followed were quite clearly a continuation of, and a substitute for, the sermons that he had been giving as a Unitarian minister (and would, in fact, go on giving for some time after his resignation). As the early sermons collected in A. C. McGiffert, Jr., *Young Emerson Speaks*, show, many of the themes and sometimes even the very words of those sermons found their way into Emerson's later lectures, essays, and books.

Nor was it only that the lecture format replaced the sermon format as Emerson's principal mode of expression and means of livelihood. The subject matter of the lectures also was pressed into service for the achievement of the same ends to which he had been addressing his preaching. And that meant, in the first instance, that he devoted his earliest lectures to the natural sciences. As the most recent biography of Emerson has put it, "It was no accident that Emerson chose natural science for his first public lectures."[2] He had, of course, never been a biblical literalist, even in his heyday as a theologian, but he found his opposition to a literal interpretation of the biblical stories of creation confirmed and even extended by his exposure to what was being unearthed by the geologists and explored by the astronomers. Although he was lecturing, in the 1830s, long before Charles Darwin (who was to die on April 19, 1882, just eight days before Emerson) would propound the *Origin of the Species*, Emerson had no need for the six days of creation in Genesis as a foundation for his understanding either of the natural world or of the place of man in it.

On the contrary, far from engaging in the steady retreat, painful inch by painful inch, by which the creationists in the nineteenth century surrendered the theological and moral territory to scientific naturalists, Emerson embraced science as the most promising of the new alternatives to theology that his age was presenting to him and his contemporaries. "Is it not a good symptom for society," he wrote to William on January 18, 1834 (*L* 1:404), "this decided & growing taste for natural science which has appeared though yet in its first gropings?" He added that he had been "writing three lectures on Natural History and of course reading as much geology, chemistry, and physics as I could find." The painstaking catalogue of the books that Emerson withdrew from libraries (prepared and published by Kenneth W. Cameron in 1941)[3] gives us an insight into the astonishing range of "reading as much as I could find," as do the many quotations and allusions that appear throughout the four lectures on science, given between November 5, 1833, and May 7, 1834. Such an interest in scientific matters went back to Emerson's childhood, when, we are told, "the outdoors was far more interesting to Ralph than the schoolroom, and this preference for nature over books would later be evidenced in his writings, in his romantic attachment to nature, and more specifically in a great curiosity about all branches of science."[4]

There is, nevertheless, something breathtakingly self-confident (perhaps one should say "self-reliant"), even presumptuous, about the picture of this ex-minister, armed with a reading knowledge that was quite catholic but also strikingly eclectic, taking it upon himself in 1833–34—the very years during which Michael Faraday was publishing his *Experimental Researches in Electricity* serially in the transactions of the Royal Society—to discuss, in one lecture per topic, the following scientific subjects: "The Uses of Natural History," "On the Relation of Man to the Globe," "Water," and "The Naturalist." (Incidentally, it will be of some interest in the present context to note that the second of these lectures, "On the Relation of Man to the Globe," was given as a "Franklin Lecture," presumably in honor of an earlier Franklin, who, you will recall, also had interest in both science and the humanities.) Emerson seems to have been conscious of the presumption involved in his topics; for it would appear to be more than the rhetorical convention when, in the opening sentence of the first lecture, he explained that "in accepting the invitation with which the Directors of this Society have honored me to introduce the course, I have followed my inclination rather than consulted my ability" (*EL* 1:5).

Yet we must pay attention, as Emerson obviously did, to the specific formulation of the title, which probably came from the society: "The *Uses* of Natural History."

For it was on what he sometimes called the "fruits" (*EL* 1:28) of science, and in his book of 1836 the "multitude of uses" (*W* 1:12), that he concentrated. The four components of that "multitude of uses" in 1836 were "commodity, beauty, language, and discipline." But it did not take the authority of Benjamin Franklin, whose name Matthew Arnold linked with that of Emerson as "the most distinctively and honorably American of your writers,"[5] to impress upon Emerson's audience in 1833 the immense practical changes that were being wrought then and there by science—or, as we would now prefer to say, by technology. The "uses" of natural history were, in the first instance, the ones that were responsible for such changes. In Emerson's words, "the history of modern times has repeatedly shown that a single man devoted to science may carry forward the mechanic arts and multiply the products of commerce more than the united population of a country can accomplish in ages wherein no particular devotion to scientific pursuits exists" (*EL* 1:12). The contributions of these "mechanic arts" could never be the whole of "the uses of natural history" for an Emerson, as we shall have opportunity to note at length in a moment, but it would be a distortion to ignore them.

Probably the most interesting of the "mechanic arts" in the thought of Emerson at this time was the art of navigation. Just four weeks before, he had returned from Great Britain on a voyage that had taken five weeks, having made the eastward transatlantic crossing also in five weeks, from December 25, 1832, to February 2, 1833. Thus he had spent almost one-fifth of the year 1833 at sea. Several years earlier he had spoken in his *Journal*, after a coastal voyage from Boston to

Charleston, about "this tent tossed on the ocean" (*JMN* 3:57); but the experience of seeing the 236-ton brig *Jasper* pointed from Boston harbor to a destination in the Azores and, sixteen days later, arriving within one mile of the master's reckoning, and that without a chronometer, made an even deeper impression on him. He referred to "the capital art of navigation of the deep sea," and ventured the characteristic suggestion that "the history of navigation affords the most striking instances . . . of the accurate adjustment of the powers of nature to the wants of man" (*EL* 1:35, 38). A sailing ship could change itself from the shape of a butterfly to that of a log, as its crew adapted it to the ever changing conditions of the weather. Emerson was clearly struck by the new possibilities being opened by the invention of the steam engine for ships, as a result of which the sailor "no longer waits for favoring gales, but by means of steam, he realizes the fable of Aeolus's bag, and carries the two and thirty winds in the boiler of his boat" (*W* 1:13); but he was not the first, nor the last, to harbor the suspicion that propulsion by means of combustion was basically against nature. (His first trip by train seems to have been the one from Manchester to Liverpool in August 1833, when he saw a train going in the opposite direction dart by "like a trout" (*JMN* 4:226).

In addition to navigation and other forms of transportation, other fields of human endeavor were the beneficiaries of the "fruits" of natural science. In the lecture "Water," which Emerson's twentieth-century editors characterize as the "most factual and least personal of his scientific talks" (*EL* 1:50), he described some recent experiments with water, from which one could begin to understand "the mode in which nature operates in regions forever hid from human sight," through what he called "the precise office performed by the pressure of great masses of water in the continual reproduction of continents" (*EL* 1:58). As he noted in the conclusion of that lecture, in words that sound more prescient of such twentieth-century developments as "heavy water" than they are, "in a bucket of water resides a latent force sufficient to counterbalance mountains, or to rend the planet" (*EL* 1:68). Some of the most celebrated "uses of natural history" were, of course, those that were appearing in medicine: not only the benefits of fresh air and exercise (*EL* 1:10–11), but the work of Edward Jenner (1749–1823), who had died only ten years earlier and whom Emerson evidently had in mind with the statement, "He has learned from the chance experience of some dairy-maids to inoculate his flesh with a disease from the udder of a cow, and by that means to defend himself from a more dangerous disease to which his own race are subject" (*EL* 1:43)—although, curiously, Emerson's only explicit reference to Jenner by name pertained to his paper "On the Migration of Birds," read in the year of his death to the Royal Society (*EL* 1:82n).

Not only because of its importance for navigation but even more for its intellectual significance, astronomy had a special "multitude of uses." "Another voyage," he said, "would make an astronomer of me" (*JMN* 4:107). Already in his sermon on astronomy, first preached on May 27, 1832, Emerson had pointed out that "the science of astronomy has had an irresistible effect in modifying and enlarging the doctrines of theology," rendering unacceptable such venerable theological notions as predestination and atonement through the blood of Christ (McGiffert, 173–77) but, in general, providing "not contradiction but correction," "not denial but purification" for the doctrines of the New Testament. "Astronomy," he summarized in his *Journal (JMN* 4:26), "proves theism, but disproves dogmatic theology. . . . It operates steadily to establish the moral laws." Now, in the Boston lectures, he called astronomy "the most perfect of the sciences" (*EL* 1:36), and it seems unavoidable to see in the famous and often ridiculed mystical passage about being "a transparent eye-ball" (in the first chapter of *Nature*) a later form of the ideas he had set forth already—twenty years earlier in the Boston Latin School—when the vision of the stars one night as he was crossing Boston Common had inspired him to compose an essay on astronomy.[6] Astronomy had a special power because it permitted Emerson to do justice to the very practical "uses of natural philosophy," and yet transcend them, by going beyond the utilitarian, and even beyond the empirical, to the *mysterium tremendum.*

The passage from Chapter 1 of *Nature*, to which I just referred, is perhaps the most luminous expression of this characteristic of Emerson's natural philosophy, and it bears quoting: "Standing on the bare ground,—my head bathed by the blithe air, and uplifted into infinite space,—all mean egotism vanishes. I become a transparent eye-ball. I am nothing. I see all. The currents of the Universal Being circulate through me; I am part or particle of God. . . . I am the lover of uncontained and immortal beauty" (*W* 1:10). One of Emerson's most discerning modern readers has called this "an image impatient with all possibility of loss" and has suggested that it is "less an image than a promise of perpetual repetition,"[7] and Sherman Paul has identified it as "justly the representative anecdote of his experience of inspiration."[8] Another context is what Emerson himself called, in his first lecture (*EL* 1:7), "a presentiment of relations to external nature, which outruns the limits of actual science." It is evident from later portions of that lecture that what he had in mind, for example, were the theories of "animal magnetism" associated with the mystical and "scientific" thought of Franz Mesmer (who had died in 1815). But Emerson had many such "presentiments of relations to external nature" that would always "outrun the limits of actual science." He found an apt word for the sum of these "presentiments" in the Greek term κόσμος.

Repeatedly—in his *Journal* and then in his lectures and then in his book *Nature* of 1836—he would turn to this word to summarize his ideas. He reminded his hearers that they were living in a period of world history that had received an "immense inheritance of natural knowledge," but was adding "great discoveries of its own," and he defined it as a duty to "avail ourselves of their light." From these new discoveries came a confirmation of ancient truth: "The eternal beauty which led the early Greeks to call the globe κόσμος or Beauty pleads ever with us, shines from the stars, glows in the flower, moves in the animal, crystallizes in the stone." Thus astronomy, biology, and geology all supported the same basic axiom. Indeed, "no truth can be more self evident than that the highest state of man, physical, intellectual, and moral can only coexist with a perfect theory of Animated Nature."[9] In *Nature,* he became more explicit in opposing this appreciation of the natu-

ral world to the vulgar utilitarianism of a purely technological or exploitative view: "The ancient Greeks
called the world κόσμος, beauty. Such is the constitution of all things, or such the plastic power of the
human eye, that the primary forms, as the sky, the
mountain, the tree, the animal, give us a delight *in and
for themselves*" (*W* 1:15; italics his). And he did this in a
chapter of *Nature* to which he gave the superscription
"Beauty," which was how he translated the Greek
word κόσμος.

The key phrase in Emerson's definition, as indicated
also by his use of italics, is "a delight in and for themselves." He would, he had confessed in his very first
lecture, be ashamed to neglect the delight that sprang
from the contemplation of a truth of nature, "in too
particular a showing what profit was to accrue from the
knowledge of nature"; for the primary axiom was:
"The knowledge itself, is the highest benefit" (*EL* 1:14).
His was no snobbish condescension to the utilitarianism of more practical men. He spoke with considerable
admiration of those who "believe that mustard bites
the tongue, that pepper is hot, friction matches incendi-
ary, revolvers are to be avoided, and suspenders hold
up pantaloons" (*W* 4:153). As James Russell Lowell
said of Emerson, "What, then, is his secret? Is it not
that he out-Yankees us all? that his range includes us
all? that he is equally at home with the potato-disease
and original sin, with pegging shoes and the Over-
soul?"[10] The difference between him and others was
that he was not content to state "what profit was to
accrue from the knowledge of nature," whether for
medicine or navigation or agriculture. Any such "profit" was a reflection of a deeper reality, of the more

fundamental laws of nature, to which the mind should address itself. "The time is not lost and the efforts not misspent," he reminded the utilitarians in the conclusion of his first lecture, "that are devoted to the elucidation of these laws; for herein is writ by the Creator his own history" (*EL* 1:26).

That unshakable conviction, to which Emerson held from this lecture to his last, also helps to account for the serene confidence that enabled him to venture into science in his early lectures and books. Indeed, "serene confidence" is the only way to describe an outlook that could assert, as he did in the introduction to the book *Nature* in 1836 (*W* 1:3): "Undoubtedly we have no questions to ask which are unanswerable." The grounds for such an assertion lay in the trust "that whatever curiosity the order of things has awakened in our minds, the order of things can satisfy." It is certainly not far-fetched to read the phrase "the order of things" as a term for God, and to see in this confidence an expression of the *analogia entis* between God and man; all our senses, and beyond the senses, the soul, are tuned to the order of things in which we live (*EL* 1:44). "It is fit," Emerson said elsewhere (*EL* 1:73), "that man should look upon Nature with the eye of the Artist, to learn from the great Artist whose blood beats in our veins, whose taste is upspringing in our own perception of beauty, the laws by which our hands should work." The analogy between God and man, then, was to be found in the artistry of God, of which our sense of the fitness of things was an image. "Our own perception of beauty" was a product and an expression of the "taste" of the great Artist, "whose blood beats in our veins." And the outcome was to be a recognition of "the laws by which our hands should work," and specifically, "that we may build St. Peter'ses or paint Transfigurations or sing Iliads in worthy continuation of the architecture of the Andes."

The beauty of the work of "the great Artist" pervaded the natural world, as Emerson had discovered both from personal observation and from his wide reading. Thus his contemporary, William Scoresby (1789–1857), a scientist, explorer, and clergyman, had, in his *An Account of the Arctic Regions and Northern Whale Fishery* (Edinburgh, 1820), presented a comparative study of snowflakes. From it, and obviously also from his own experience, Emerson had learned that "whilst the angles of the primitive crystal of the snowflake are invariable there is yet the greatest *variety and beauty* in the forms in which secondary crystals radiate from these" (*EL* 1:64). In the same lecture on "Water," Emerson also took occasion to note that "the annual formation and destruction of ice within the Arctic Circle is a beautiful provision of Nature for mitigating the excessive inequality of temperature" (*EL* 1:59). Fresh from his own voyages and from the travelogues he had read, he reflected on "the decoration of the Globe" as this "decoration" was distributed across different regions, so that one part of the world had the Southern Cross and another Niagara (*EL* 1:41–42). The most minute grain of sand, as disclosed through "the microscope and the laws of polarization and chemistry," had "a life as large as yours" (*EL* 1:77–78). Indeed, "there is no object so foul that intense light will not make it beautiful" (*W* 1:15).

All these natural beauties, then, were "a delight in and for themselves" (*W* 1:15), and that insight was fundamental to the natural sciences. Practicality there was and must be, but "not only a relation of use but a relation of beauty subsists between man himself and nature, *which leads him to Science"* (*EL* 1:48). While one must hesitate for fear of pressing Emerson's formulas into a literal precision that would be alien to his very spirit, he does appear to be saying that the relation between beauty and science was one in which the science was derivative from, and dependent upon, the sense of beauty—even though there was, of course, also a sense in which the discoveries of science led to beauty. From Goethe, to whom we shall turn in more detail later, Emerson had learned to say that "the works of nature are ever a freshly uttered Word of God." Goethe's aphorism prompted him to add: "Perhaps it is the province of poetry rather than of prose to describe the effect upon the mind and heart of these nameless influences. Certainly he that has formed his ideas of adaptation of beauty on these models can have nothing mean in his estimate" (*EL* 1:72–73).

Yet the basic principle of "delight in and for themselves" was directed against crude utilitarianism, not against subjectivity. On the contrary, Emerson insisted over and over that there must be a reciprocal relation between the design and beauty of the natural world and the eye of the beholder. "It is certain," he stated in the first chapter of *Nature*, "that the power to produce this delight, does not reside in nature, but in man," and then, as if to correct himself, he added, "or in a harmony of both" (*W* 1:11). This notion of harmony, or as he sometimes called it "proportion," was both: a predicate of the natural world, seen as κόσμος or beauty, and a predicate of man. In the dithyrambic peroration of his lecture "On the Relation of Man to the Globe," Emerson exclaimed: "An equal symmetry and proportion is discoverable between man and the air, the mountains, the tides, the moon and the sun. I am not impressed by solitary marks of designing wisdom; I am thrilled with delight by the choral harmony of the whole. Design! It is all design. It is all beauty. It is all astonishment" (*EL* 1:49). Another word, in addition to κόσμος, beauty, design, and proportion, was "fitness": "It only needs to have the eye informed, to make everything we see, every plant, every spider, every moss, every patch of mould upon the bark of a tree, give us the idea of fitness" (*EL* 1:17). And the "link" between these creatures, the "secret sympathy," was "the Mind of Man," who "marries the visible to the Invisible by uniting thought to Animal Organisation" (*EL* 1:24).

Emerson began the substantive part of his first lecture, after the customary *captatio benevolentiae*, with the topic sentence: "It seems to have been designed if anything was, that men should be students of Natural History" (*EL* 1:6). And despite the statement, in this lecture (*EL* 1:10) and in his *Journal* (*JMN* 4:200), "I will be a naturalist," there was no possibility of his becoming an experimental scientist. If Emerson became a "naturalist," it had to be in the spirit he articulated in the fourth chapter of *Nature* (*W* 1:26): "Every natural fact is a symbol of some spiritual fact," because to Emerson "it is not only words that are emblematic; it is things which are emblematic." A study of the several natural sciences would show that man "had been prophesied in nature for a thousand ages before he appeared" (*EL* 1:29). The subject matter of these sciences, therefore, was a "delight" for its own sake—but also a "delight" to man. Therefore, the study of nature and the study of man belonged together, by reason of the "proportion" or "fitness" or "beauty" that was in both. Quoting some lines from Wordsworth (whom he had visited at Rydal Mount a few months earlier [*JMN* 4:222–23]), Emerson asked: "Can the effect be other than most beneficent upon the faculties dedicated to such observations?—upon the man given

> To reverent watching of each still report
> That Nature utters from her rural shrine."[11]

That stress upon the "beneficent effect" of the study of nature represented an awareness, to which Emerson gave repeated expression, that such concepts as "delight" or "κόσμος=Beauty" could lead to a grave misunderstanding. In his study of Vladimir Nabokov, significantly entitled *Escape into Aesthetics*, Professor Page Stegner has said of Nabokov: "Even though he may make a religion of form, value beauty more than truth, he does not *confuse* art and life. Design, it is true, is everything for Nabokov. Quality, style, beauty are substituted, actually, for morality in his novels."[12] That is a judgment to which Emerson would likewise appear to be liable, along with his friend and mentor Coleridge and their great contemporary Schleiermacher, and many other so-called Romantics. Sherman Paul, who has shown how profound was the affinity between Emerson and Coleridge, has also provided us with a helpful definition of "beauty" in Emerson's thought: "Beauty is the result of seeing beyond illusions by means of one's spiritual center or reliance."[13] It was not an illusion, but a cure for illusion; and it was not an "escape into aesthetics," but a profoundly moral and an authentically humanizing force.

"Beauty in nature is not ultimate," Emerson warned. "It is the herald of inward and eternal beauty" (*W* 1:24). But that "inward beauty" was not a self-indulgent aestheticism, according to Emerson. Because "truth, and goodness, and beauty, are but different faces of the same All" (ibid.), the beauty of nature and the beauty of art must serve the formation of character. It was, moreover, the "progress of Natural Science" that was promoting such a sense of beauty and, hence, such a formation of character, by developing "new and great lessons of which good men shall understand the moral" (*EL* 1:26). That was evident in the career of scientists. On the last page of his sermon "Summer," first preached on June 14, 1829 (although this note probably came later), Emerson wrote: "Addenda. All students of natural science simple and amiable men; not petulant like men of letters" (McGiffert, 222). He was, he said in a lecture (*EL* 1:22–23), impressed by "the narrative of sleepless nights, laborious days and dangerous journeyings" in the life of scientists, "this high unconditional devotion to their cause, this trampling under foot of every thing pitiful and selfish in the zeal of their pursuit of nature"—more impressed, in fact, by "this development of character" than by the scientific discoveries themselves.

"Development of character," then, was the deeper— and more important—substratum of science and of beauty. Emerson wanted to "learn the law of the diffraction of a ray," he said in his *Journal* (JMN 4:322), "because, when I understand it, it will illustrate, perhaps suggest a new truth in ethics."

Having discoursed on the advantages of country life over city life because of the beauties that the countryside exhibited, in winter no less than in summer, Emerson reminded his readers that even the beauty of a New England autumn or of the moon was not enough: "The presence of a higher, namely, of the spiritual element is essential to its perfection. The high and divine beauty . . . is that which is found in combination with the human will, and never separate." And then came the canonical axiom: "Beauty is the mark God sets upon virtue" (*W* 1:19). Every heroic act was also decent, and conversely, no act that violated decency or neglected virtue could be either heroic or beautiful. It was only "a virtuous man" who could be "the central figure of the visible sphere" (*W* 1:22). From these admonitions it is evident that Emerson recognized the potential dangers of aestheticism that lurked in his lyrical celebration of the beauties of nature, and that he was sensitive to the charge (frequently levelled against him, especially in the controversy over the abolition of slavery) that his aestheticism was self-indulgent and morally sterile.

Therefore: "Natural history by itself has no value; it is like a single sex. But marry it to human history, & it is poetry" (*JMN* 4:311). He recognized not only the dangers of aestheticism, but also what he called "the evils of Science," against which it was necessary to "guard" by "recurring to Nature" (*EL* 1:76). But the way to "recur to Nature" was by "marrying" natural history to human history. Significantly, when he spoke about the "development of character" that had been at work in the "high unconditional devotion of scientists to their cause" and in "the zeal of their pursuit of nature," it

was to "the biography of chemists, botanists, physi- /
cians, geometers" that he specifically referred (*EL*
1:22–23). That was in his first lecture, on November 5,
1833. And so it ought not to be a surprise that Emerson, after launching his career as a lecturer with four
discourses on the sciences, should have turned to biography. In turn, it ought not to be a surprise that Emerson, in his lectures and writings on biography, continued to sound many of the themes that had been his
leitmotiv from the beginning. For, as he said in the
fourth chapter of *Nature*, "the laws of moral nature
answer to those of matter as face to face in a glass" (*W*
1:32–33). It is, then, from Emerson on natural history
and "the Uses of Natural History" to biography in
Emerson and "The Uses of Great Men" that I shall turn
in my second lecture.

II. "The Uses of Great Men"

Ralph Waldo Emerson made his mark in our history
chiefly as a lecturer and an author: he began his career
as a platform speaker with a series of public presenta-
tions in Boston in the autumn of 1833 and into 1834,
all of which dealt with one or another aspect of the
natural sciences; and he launched the other phase of
his public vocation in 1836, with the publication
(anonymous, although he did not try to keep it secret)
of a book bearing the title *Nature*.

Yet it is, of course, not as a scientist, nor even as a
popularizer and interpreter of science, that he is known
and remembered a century after his death, but as a
philosopher of humanity. And although what Bliss Per-

ry once called "Emerson's Most Famous Speech"[14] was the Phi Beta Kappa address at Harvard on August 31, 1837, entitled "The American Scholar," which Oliver Wendell Holmes hailed as "our intellectual Declaration of Independence," it was in fact with biography that Emerson made the transition from the philosophy of science to the philosophy of humanity. For he believed, as he wrote in his *Journal* (and would repeat several times in the following years), that "natural history by itself has no value; it is like a single sex. But marry it to human history, & it is poetry" (*JMN* 4:311). Those words from the *Journal*, which have provided the theme for these Franklin Lectures, are the ones of which Emerson's original editor, his son Edward Waldo, was reminded and which he quoted as a commentary on his father's words in the first chapter of *Representative Men* (*W* 4:10): "Something is wanting to science until it has been humanized." It would seem that we have a right to be reminded of them as well when, in his early lecture on "The Naturalist," Emerson drew a contrast between the "poet," who "loses himself in imaginations and for want of accuracy is a mere fabulist," and the "savant," who, "losing sight of the end of his inquiries in the perfection of his manipulations becomes an apothecary, a pedant"; "it is," Emerson said, "for want of this marriage that both remain unfruitful" (*EL* 1:79). The same passage comes to mind when Emerson describes Plato as "this well-bred all-knowing Greek geometer" at the same time as "the Euclid of holiness" who "marries the two parts of nature" (*W* 4:87).

In spite of the polemic against the "want of accuracy" that was the occupational disease of the poet, it is evident from these passages, and others like them, that while Emerson was quite sincere in his strong affirmations about science, he was also extremely critical of the attempt to study "natural history" without "human history"—more critical, it would seem than of the study of "human history" without "natural history"— even though his philosophy required both. Well before he had delivered the talk on the American scholar, he saw "the study of Natural History" as a possible "cure" for the intellectual dominance of England over American thought (*EL* 1:75), and in the same lecture he spoke hopefully about "the intellectual influences of Natural Science" (*EL* 1:70). But, as he said in his first lecture, "the greatest office of natural science (and one which as yet is only begun to be discharged)" was "to explain man to himself," because "the knowledge of all the facts of all the laws of nature will give man his true place in the system of being" (*EL* 1:23). Even astronomy, whose "irresistible effect in modifying and enlarging the doctrines of theology" he had praised in an early sermon (McGiffert, 173–177) and which he regarded as "the most perfect of the sciences" (*EL* 1:46), had to meet this definition of the greatest office of natural science: "it must come up into life to have its full value, and not remain there in globes and spaces" (*W* 4:110). Plato, in the *Republic,* therefore, "may be said to require and so to anticipate the astronomy of Laplace" (*W* 4:82).

The overarching category comprehending both science and the humanities was, for Emerson, the concept "nature," which was the title of his first book, published in 1836, as well as of the essay (*W* 3:167–96) that "contains the philosophical assumptions of the

Second Series" of *Essays,* published in 1844.[15] From the
beginning, he maintained that "the whole of Nature is
a metaphor or image of the human Mind" (*EL* 1:24),
which could as well have been inverted to read: "The
human Mind is a metaphor or image of the whole of
Nature"; for the two sentences would mean the same.
The distinction between "mind" and "nature" was the
distinction between the one and the many. The spec-
ulations of the mind led "to a terrific unity, in which all
things are absorbed"; by contrast, "nature is the manifold" (*W* 4:51). There was in nature nothing "false or
unsuccessful" (*EL* 1:72), and this, too, was a metaphor
for the human mind when it was authentic and true to
itself. "A man," said Emerson in the introductory chapter of *Representative Men* (*W* 4:9), "is a center for nature,
running out threads of relation through every thing,
fluid and solid, material and elemental." Therefore the
fundamental assumption was the continuity between
man and nature, as between the one and the many, in
fact the continuity even between "the secret of heav-
en," which was unknown and unknowable to the very
saints, and "the best in nature," with which it had to
"tally" (*W* 4:140–41).

It was in this context of his concept of "nature" that
Emerson spoke of "marrying" natural history to
human history, and it was on this basis that he articulated not only his philosophy of the natural sciences,
but his philosophy of the human sciences, too, since
these as well were of course "natural sciences" according to his definition of "nature." That presupposition
had a pronounced effect on Emerson's conception of
human history, for which nature was not so much the
antithesis (despite the antithetical-sounding formula-

tions) as the matrix. One could, therefore, see the greatness of Plato in this, that "he domesticates the soul in nature: man is the microcosm" (*W* 4:86). Now what did all of this imply for human history? Emerson's answer, in the second paragraph of the first chapter of *Representative Men* (*W* 4:3), was "Nature seems to exist for the excellent." Later in the same chapter, he propounded the thesis (to which I shall return) that "within the limits of human education and agency, we may say that great men exist that there may be greater men," citing in substantiation of the thesis the general principle that "the destiny of organized nature is amelioration, and who can tell its limits?" (*W* 4:35). Nature, he speculated in a later chapter of the same series (significantly, the one on Goethe), had it as an aim to inspire in man an imitation of it, but such "imitative expression" was "mere stenography." Beyond mere stenography were "higher degrees" of expression, and nature had reserved "more splendid endowments for those whom she elects to a superior office." These were the "scholars and writers," for "Nature has nearly at heart the formation of the speculative man, or scholar" (*W* 4:264). In the production of the scholar or writer, therefore, "Nature conspires" (*W* 4:263–64).

After his lectures on natural history in late 1833 and early 1834, Emerson's focus moved more and more to human history, to which he devoted six lectures, beginning on January 29, 1835. Unfortunately, we do not have the text of the introductory lecture in the series, which is variously referred to as "Tests of Great Men" or as "The Study and Uses of Biography" (*EL* 1:97). Ten years later, he called the introductory lecture of *Representative Men* "Uses of Great Men," thus combining the two versions of the earlier title. For our purposes here, it is more significant that "Uses of Great Men" seems to be an echo, perhaps even an intentional echo, of the "Uses of Natural History," on which Emerson had lectured in his first platform appearance on November 5, 1833. Intentional or not, "Uses of Great Men" demonstrates what happened in Emerson's philosophy when natural history was married to human history.

"Emerson's theory of human greatness," John O. McCormick has observed, "plagued him all his life. He began his formulation in boyhood, he struggled with it throughout his manhood, and while *Representative Men* gave him a limited satisfaction, he continued to review various aspects of the formulation—political, historical, and metaphysical—until senescence."[16] From the *Journals* and other writings of the late 1830s and early 1840s, the years between the first lectures on biography and *Representative Men* (delivered as lectures in December 1845 and January 1846, and eventually published on January 1, 1850), Henry Nash Smith has compiled a roster of the appellations for the great man that Emerson employed: "the contemplative man, the man of genius, the scholar, the torch-bearer, the seer, the saint, the dissenter, the aspirant, the radical, the spiritualist, the idealist, the Transcendentalist, the hero."[17] This was the man whom "Nature conspired" to make possible, whom Nature "elects to a superior office" by conferring on him "more splendid endowments," the "excellent" for whom "Nature seems to exist."

The five great men presented in the 1835 series of lectures were Michel Angelo [*sic*] Buonarroti, Martin Luther, John Milton, George Fox, Edmund Burke. The series of 1845/1846, on the other hand, presented six great men, none of them repeated from the earlier catalogue: Plato, Swedenborg, Montaigne, Shakspeare [*sic*], Napoleon, Goethe. What did these eleven men have in common? Then again, what did they *not* have in common? To begin with the obvious, which is perhaps not so obvious, all of them were what Emerson called "men of large calibre"; it was characteristic of such men, he said, that even though they might be afflicted with "some eccentricity or madness," they "help us more [or, in the title of his introductory chapter, are of more "use"] than balanced mediocre minds" (*W* 4:99). The qualification about "some eccentricity or madness" (in connection with which he cited only the examples of Pascal and Newton—both of them, interestingly, scientists but also philosophers) is an important one, because it enabled Emerson to identify someone as a "great man" without having to describe him as admirable in every aspect of his life. In his *Journal* for 1832 (*JMN* 4:35), he had criticized his predecessors in the field of biography on the grounds that "they that have writ the lives of great men have not written them from love & from seeing the beauty that was to be desired in them." He wrote this as part of the observation that a "modern Plutarch" had not yet appeared, and before he had become well acquainted with the writings of Thomas Carlyle, whose *Heroes and Hero-Worship* was, in any case, not to be published until 1841. Even in 1832, Emerson clearly purposed, when he would write the lives of great men, to do so "from love" and "from seeing the beauty that was to be desired in them."

Whatever this beauty was, it was a common property

of all truly great men. "Does it not seem," Emerson wrote elsewhere in his *Journal* (*JMN* 4:336), "as if a perfect parallelism [an allusion to Plutarch's *Parallel Lives*?] existed between every great & fully developed man & every other?" Conversely, these qualities, whatever they were, were not—or, at least, not at first sight—the common property of all men, great or less than great. "I count him a great man," he said near the beginning of "Uses of Great Men," "who inhabits a higher sphere of thought, into which other men rise with labor and difficulty" (*W* 4:6). And near the end of the lecture he spoke of the great man as "an exponent of a vaster mind and will" (*W* 4:34–35). The labor and difficulty that hindered other men from rising to that "higher sphere of thought" Emerson frequently contrasted with what he called "genius." "Genius" he defined as "the naturalist or geographer of the supersensible regions, which draws their map" (*W* 4:16). And in a formulation that cannot help but remind us of Carlyle (whom by the time of *Representative Men* he had not only read with great devotion, but had visited at his farm, "Craigenputtock," in the Scottish moors, during his pilgrimage to the British Isles, on August 25, 1833), Emerson declared: "The genius of humanity is the right point of view of history" (*W* 4:33). In a later aphorism, drawing the distinction of genius and talent which becomes increasingly important to him, he asserted: "The failure of genius is better than the victories of talent."[18]

One characteristic that many or all of the eleven "great men" of the two series shared was their willingness to break with a dead past. Luther, for example, stood "in glaring contrast" with the "imitative and artificial"; he "abhorred dependence" of his time, or of any time, on the institutions and ideas that had been handed down (*EL* 1:142). Emerson had long cherished a deep antipathy to the tyranny of the past. He had opened his first book (*Nature,* published in 1836) with an attack on this tyranny. "Our age is retrospective," he said in the very first sentence. While "the foregoing generations beheld God and nature face to face," it was typical of this "retrospective age" that it "builds the sepulchres of the fathers" and that it saw God and nature not "face to face," but through the eyes of the past. Yet, Emerson asked defiantly, "Why should not we also enjoy an original relation to the universe?" Or, putting the antithesis even more explicitly, he continued, "Why should not we have a poetry and philosophy of *insight* and not of *tradition*?" (*W* 1:3; my italics). His readiness to break with tradition in the name of insight had led him, on October 28, 1832, to resign from the pastorate of Second Church in Boston and, in fact, from the Unitarian ministry altogether, citing his conviction that, despite a tradition that even Unitarians continued to honor, he could no longer celebrate the Lord's Supper. For, he explained, "it is not usage . . . that binds me to [Christianity]. . . . That form out of which the life and suitableness have departed should be as worthless in [faith's] eyes as the dead leaves that are falling around us" (*W* 11:21).

In the most famous (or infamous) statement of the antithesis, the Divinity School Address of 1838, he denounced those who "have come to speak of the revelation as somewhat long ago given and done, as if God were dead. . . . to speak as books enable, as synods use, as the fashion guides, and as interest commands" (*W* 1:134–35), by contrast with "the true preacher, who can be known by this, that he deals out to the people his life—life passed through thc firc of thought" (*W* 1:138). It remained true, he complained, "that tradition characterizes the preaching of this country; that it comes out of the memory, and not out of the soul" (*W* 1:141). "Memory" versus "soul" in the Divinity School Address, or "tradition" versus "insight" in the *Nature* of 1836, or "Man Thinking" versus "the parrot of other men's thinking" in "The American Scholar" (*W* 1:84)—this was an opposition throughout the history of thought and the history of society. Therefore, one of the most important among the "uses of great men" was to help shatter the tyranny of the traditional. When genius did its work properly, Emerson said in *Representative Men* (*W* 4:16), it would "cool our affection for the old" by "acquainting us with new fields of activity," and this was what the great men of the past had done. All the more ironic was it, therefore, that these same great men should so often have been enshrined as part of a tradition that would go on to tyrannize succeeding generations. The most flagrant example was, of course, what had been done to Jesus. "Alone in all history he estimated the greatness of man. One man was true to what is in you and me," Emerson said in the Divinity School Address (*W* 1:128); but now "churches are not built on his principles, but on his tropes" and on his figurative language, as though it were literal prose (*W* 1:129).

The seeming inevitability of this process of distortion, by which the liberating insight of the great men during one generation was turned into the suffocating tradition of the next generation, may well be inherent in the very concept of "the great man." Emerson was not insensitive to that danger, nor to the other dangers of his theme. In fact, there is a remarkable brief passage in the first chapter of *Representative Men* (*W* 4:31) in which he cited three fundamental dangers: "But *great men* [italics his]: — the word is injurious. Is there caste? Is there fate? What becomes of the promise to virtue?" The three dangers may be formulated as the relation of the great man to the common man, the relation of greatness to fate and free will, and the relation of greatness to morality.

"Is there caste?" Emerson asked. If a great man was one "who inhabits a higher sphere of thought, into which other men rise with labor and difficulty" (*W* 4:6), what did that leave for these "other men"? Without engaging in the discussion of whether Emerson's doctrine of great men is some kind of proto-fascism,[19] one must deal with the question of "caste"; and Emerson did. He identified it as a danger that "appears in the excess of influence of the great man," that such a man by "his attraction warps us from our place," with the result that "we have become underlings and intellectual suicides" (*W* 4:27). He sought to counteract the danger by invoking the distinction cited earlier between "genius" and mere "talent." It was, he said, "the delight of vulgar talent to dazzle and to blind the beholder," which was what made the beholder, as he said, an underling and an intellectual suicide. By contrast, however, "true genius seeks to defend us from itself" (*W* 4:18). And in one way or another, that was a characteristic of all of Emerson's "great men." It was, he said in the lecture on Swedenborg (*W* 4:143), "the best sign of a great nature that it opens a foreground, and, like the breath of morning landscapes, invites us onward." Thus Plato, out of whom had come "all things that are still written and debated among men of thought" (*W* 4:49), opened such a foreground; for "when we are exalted by ideas, we do not owe this to Plato, but to the idea, to which also Plato was debtor" (*W* 4:19). Or Luther, by whom Emerson was fascinated and yet puzzled, or even repelled, was proof that "the greatest men are precisely those whose characters are easy to understand," because "those talents and means which operate great results on society, are those which are common to all men" (*EL* 1:119). That was what made great men a "collyrium to clear our eyes" (*W* 4:25), by pointing beyond themselves to what Emerson in his essay on "History" called the "one mind common to all individual men" (*W* 2:3).

"Is there caste? Is there fate?" On hearing Emerson use the word "fate" in a lecture given in 1845, anyone who has read extensively in him must be reminded of a passage in his *Journal*, written in January 1842 upon the death of his five-year-old son Waldo, whom his father mourned until his own death (among his last recorded words are "Oh that beautiful boy!"). My friend and colleague Harold Bloom has spoken of being "haunted" by this passage, which he calls "the epitome of the glory and sorrows of Emerson, and of our American Romanticism."[20] And since I, too, have always been "haunted" by it, I shall, despite its length, quote it in full (*JMN* 8:228):

> In short, there ought to be no such thing as Fate. As long as we use this word, it is a sign of our impotence & that we are not yet ourselves. There is now a sublime revelation in each of us which makes us so strangely

aware & certain of our riches that although I have never since I was born for so much as one moment expressed the truth, and although I have never heard the expression of it from any other, I know that the whole is here, — the wealth of the Universe is for me, everything is explicable & practicable for me.

And yet whilst I adore this ineffable life which is at my heart, it will not condescend to gossip with me, it will not announce to me any particulars of science, it will not enter into the details of my biography, & say to me why I have a son and daughters born to me, or why my son dies in his sixth year of joy. Herein then I have this latent omniscience coexistent with omni-ignorance. Moreover, whilst this Deity glows at the heart, & by his unlimited presentiments gives me all Power, I know that tomorrow will be as this day, I am a dwarf, & I remain a dwarf. That is to say, I believe in Fate. As long as I am weak, I shall talk of Fate; whenever the God fills me with his fulness, I shall see the disappearance of Fate.

I am *Defeated* all the time; yet to Victory I am born.

Emerson's question, "Is there fate?" was therefore wrung out of this crushing experience, in which he learned that he was existentially a "dwarf," but that he could look to the "great men" (the greatest of whom was, for Emerson, the man Jesus, "the only soul in history who has appreciated the worth of man" [*W* 1:130]) to stand as signs, by a "sublime revelation," of "this ineffable life," which was "the wealth of the Universe." For then "the opaque self becomes transparent with the light of the First Cause."

"Is there caste? Is there fate?" And the third question was: "What becomes of the promise to virtue?" In an entry in his *Journal* (*JMN* 5:11) on "the value of Biography," Emerson had listed, among other such values, that "we can find . . . our moral judgments more truly matched in an ancient . . . than in our own family." Here, in *Representative Men*, he often returned to the consideration of that "value," recognizing the potential conflict between it and his definition of greatness. Thus he opened the chapter on "Montaigne; or, the Skeptic" with the observation: "Every fact is related on one side to sensation, and on the other to morals. The game of thought is, on the appearance of one of these sides, to find the other" (*W* 4:149). That was also the "game" of biography or human history: when "sensation" appeared, to find morals, or, as Emerson often called it, "the moral sentiment," and, on the other hand, when the moral sentiment appeared in a great man, even in an austere or rigid form, to cherish it and to "find the other side" of the man. Swedenborg, for example, was in many ways an austere and rigid man, whose "theological bias" had "fatally narrowed his interpretation of nature" and hence of sensation, and had prevented him from attaining "the liberality of universal wisdom," so that "with him . . . we are always in a church" (*W* 4:134). Nevertheless, anyone who turned the coin over and looked at the other side, according to the rules of "the game of thought," would discover "the moral insight of Swedenborg, the correction of popular errors, the announcement of ethical laws," all of which, for Emerson, "take him out of comparison with any other modern writer" (*W* 4:124). By contrast, Plato lacked "the vital authority" that had expressed itself in "the screams of prophets" (*W* 4:75–76), and to get at his "moral sentiment" it was necessary to go through the "intellectual" and "literary" forms of his thought.

This difficulty with "the promise to virtue" and "the moral sentiment" in the uses of great men was the counterpart, within human history, of the requirement in the uses of natural history to recognize "development of character" in the career of the scientist (*EL* 1:22–23) and to seek that "inward and eternal beauty" of which "beauty in nature" was only "the herald" (*W* 1:24). For as it was true in natural history that "the laws of moral nature answer to those of matter as face to face in a glass," so it was in human history; in fact, that very sentence appears verbatim both in the biographical lecture on Shakespeare of December 10, 1835 (*EL* 1:290) and in the fourth chapter of *Nature* in 1836 (*W* 1:32–33). It acted as a corrective, to offset the amoral or even immoral implications of aesthetic "sensation" and of heroic "greatness." Now "sensation" and "the moral sentiment" may have been, for Emerson, the two sides of the same coin, but that did not make them equal. The moral dimension of reality had an ultimacy of claim, to which all else must yield; for "whenever the sentiment of right comes in, it takes precedence of every thing else. For other things, I make poetry of them; but the moral sentiment makes poetry of me" (*W* 4:93–94). And so, while it was true that "society has really no graver interest than the well-being of the literary class," which made the scholar and writer "the man of the ages," it was necessary to remind him that he must at the same time "stand well with his contemporaries" (*W* 4:269, 265).

That warning was sounded in the seventh and final chapter of *Representative Men*, which bore the title

"Goethe; or, the Writer." Goethe and Napoleon were the only two of the eleven great men treated in Emerson's two series of lectures who were at all his contemporaries: Napoleon died when Emerson was about to turn eighteen; but Goethe did not die until Emerson was nearly thirty, and he had received Waldo's brother William in October 1824 at Weimar. Goethe and Napoleon were also the two great men among the eleven who created the greatest problem for Emerson's insistence on the moral criterion of greatness. Napoleon was "an experiment, under the most favorable conditions, of the powers of intellect without conscience" (*W* 4:257). Goethe was in many ways even more of a problem on this count than Napoleon. The reason was, quite simply, what Emerson, in a letter to Carlyle (dated November 20, 1834) called "his misfortune, with conspicuous bad influence on his genius, — that velvet life he led." Almost apologetically but quite candidly, he acknowledged: "The Puritan in me accepts no apology for bad morals in such as *he*," and he explained: "Genius pampered, acknowledged, crowned, can only retain our sympathy by turning the same force once expended against outward enemies now against inward." In 1836 he was still referring to Goethe as "wise, but sensual," and expressing his suspicion "that under his faith is no-faith, — that under his love is love-of-ease." But he had to add that "his mind [is] as Catholic as ever any was."[21] When he came to this final chapter of *Representative Men,* he still found Goethe's *Wilhelm Meister,* which Carlyle had translated into English and which Emerson had discussed with Carlyle during their first meeting, "a very provoking book to the curiosity of young men of genius, but a very unsatisfactory one" (*W*

4:278). The basic problem with the book, and with Goethe, was that Goethe had not "worshipped the [very] highest unity," because he was "incapable of a self-surrender to the moral sentiment" (*W* 4:284).

"The foundation of culture, as of character," Emerson said in a lecture on "Progress of Culture" (*W* 8:228), "is at last the moral sentiment." Measured by that criterion, Goethe, the high priest of culture who was even devoted "to truth [only] for the sake of culture" (*W* 4:284), did not measure up; and neither, of course, did Napoleon. In preparing the lectures of 1835 on biography, Emerson had considered the inclusion of Napoleon and Goethe (*EL* 1:95), but had rejected them. By the time of the 1845/1846 lectures, however, he had decided to devote a lecture to each of them, back to back: "Bonaparte as a representative of the popular external life and aims of the nineteenth century" and Goethe as "a man quite domesticated in the century . . . and taking away, by his colossal parts, the reproach of weakness which but for him would lie on the intellectual works of the period" (*W* 4:270). It was for the sake of being able to read Goethe that Emerson taught himself German; and when Moncure Conway visited him in May 1853, he saw two statuettes of Goethe on Emerson's mantel. Emerson had come to know Goethe in part through Carlyle, but his ideas were being widely circulated; indeed, Frothingham goes so far as to say that "no author occupied the cultivated New England mind as much as [Goethe] did."[22] McCormick has used the evolution of Emerson's attitude to Goethe as a case study for the problem of the "great men," and I do not need to repeat his findings here.[23] But it is remarkable that neither McCormick nor, as far as I can tell, any other Emerson scholar has treated the importance of Goethe for the specific issue with which I am concerned in these lectures, the relation of "natural history" to "human history."

Yet, among the eleven "great men," Goethe was the one who had uniquely addressed this relation. Emerson was deeply impressed—in fact, overawed, as well he might be—by the universality of Goethe's interests and competencies. In the context of the nineteenth century, "he was the soul of his century." For if the nineteenth century had become "one great Exploring Expedition, accumulating a glut of facts and fruits too fast for any hitherto existing savans [*sic*] to classify," that did not daunt Goethe: "this man's mind had ample chambers for the distribution of all" (*W* 4:273). There was "nothing he had not the right to know . . . , no weapon in the armory of universal genius he did not take into his hand" (*W* 4:284). Goethe "found himself the master of histories, philosophies, sciences and national literatures . . . geology, chemistry, astronomy" (*W* 4:272). By contrast with earlier ages, the modern period was the time of "a multitude of things, which is distracting," but "Goethe was the philosopher of this multiplicity; hundred-handed, Argus-eyed, able and happy to cope with this rolling miscellany of facts and sciences, and by his own versatility to dispose of them with ease. . . . He . . . was born with a free and controlling genius" (*W* 4:271). With a mixture of admiration and envy, perhaps even with a touch of incredulity at the sheer size of this man, Emerson exclaimed (*W* 4:275, 272): "He sees at every pore!" Although the rubric of the seventh chapter of *Representative Men* was "the writer" (Shakespeare having preempted the title "the poet" in the fifth chapter and Plato the title "the philosopher" in the second), it might also have been called "the natural philosopher" or "the scientist." For Emerson found it possible to declare quite flatly: "He has said the best things about nature that ever were said" (*W* 4:275); and again: "The old Eternal Genius who built the world has confided himself more to this man than to any other" (*W* 4:283). Goethe had "suggested the leading idea of modern botany . . . osteology . . . optics" (*W* 4:275). He had, without any painful self-consciousness, devoted "the historical part of his Theory of Colors" to "the relation betwixt these grandees of European scientific history and himself; the mere drawing of the lines from Goethe to Kepler, from Goethe to Bacon, from Goethe to Newton" (*W* 4:287). Rudolf Magnus and, after Magnus, my late colleague Heinrich Henel have examined in some detail the specific work of Goethe as "*Naturforscher*" in various fields, especially the ones Emerson listed: botany, osteology, and optics—as well as, for example, meteorology, where he "laid the groundwork for the close network of weather stations that now covers all civilized countries."[24] Had he done nothing more, Goethe would deserve a major place in intellectual history merely for his contributions to the rise of modern science.

But he had, of course, done vastly more. The full context of Emerson's statement that Goethe had "said the best things about nature that ever were said," is: "He has defined art, its scope and laws. He has said the best things about nature that ever were said. He treats nature as the old philosophers, as the seven wise masters did, — and, with whatever loss of French tabulation and dissection, *poetry and humanity* remain to us. . . . He has contributed a key to many parts of nature, through the rare turn for unity and simplicity in his mind" (*W* 4:275; my italics). If, as Emerson maintained in the lecture on Plato (*W* 4:51), the observation of nature led to "the manifold" while the speculation of the mind led to "a terrific unity," Goethe had managed, by this "rare turn for unity and simplicity in his mind," to combine an observation that "seems to see out of every pore of his skin" with an awareness of the One and the All. As early as his lecture on Michelangelo of February 5, 1835 (*EL* 1:101), Emerson had quoted Goethe's statement of this combination: "All particular beauties scattered up and down in nature, are only so far beautiful as they suggest more or less in themselves this entire circuit of harmonious proportions." Now, in the final paragraph of *Representative Men*, summarizing his appreciation of the marriage of natural history and human history in Goethe and in his poetry, he drew from Goethe the lesson that "we too must write Bibles, *to unite again the heavens and the earthly world*" (*W* 4:290; my italics).

He was, in many ways, summarizing the *leitmotiv* of the entire book—in fact, of much of his life: "to unite again the heavens and the earthly world." His early study of natural history could not be content with the meticulous analysis of the phenomena of "the earthly world," but "Nature" had to carry him beyond the empirical, as the book of 1836 demonstrated. His study of theology—specifically, his research and reflection on the person of Jesus Christ, whom traditional Christian dogma had described as having "united again the heavens and the earthly world"—led him to the conclusion, sounded forth in the Divinity School Address of 1838, that the Jesus of Christian tradition could not unite them because, in the deepest sense, he did not belong to either one. Even his study of great men, in 1835 and again in 1845, had to transcend the details of biography to find the great man as an "effect" rather than a "cause," as "an exponent of a vaster mind and will" (*W* 4:34–35). None of these ways of knowing was adequate "to unite again the heavens and the earthly world." That could be done only if what man had put asunder could once again be joined together, as God had intended: the "uses of natural history" and the "uses of great men." For "Natural history by itself has no value; it is like a single sex. But marry it to human history, & it is poetry."

And that is precisely what he did.

Notes

1. At the suggestion of the hosts for the Franklin Lectures (and in keeping with the precedent of Emerson himself), I have endeavored in this published version to keep as much as possible of the flavor of the lecture format, instead of transforming the lectures into a small monograph (which I do, however, plan to do eventually). To that end, I have incorporated most of my citations into the text, using the following sigla:

EL   Ralph Waldo Emerson, *Early Lectures*, edited by Stephen E. Whicher and Robert E. Spiller. 2 vols. Cambridge, Mass.: Harvard University Press, 1961–64.

JMN   Ralph Waldo Emerson, *Journals and Miscellaneous Notebooks*, edited by William H. Gilman and others. 14 vols. Cambridge, Mass.: Harvard University Press, 1960–78.

L *The Letters of Ralph Waldo Emerson*, edited by Ralph L. Rusk. 6 vols. New York: Columbia University Press, 1939.

McGiffert A. C. McGiffert, Jr., editor, *Young Emerson Speaks.* Boston: Houghton Mifflin, 1938.

W *Emerson's Complete Works.* 12 vols. Boston: Houghton Mifflin, 1903–04.

2. Gay Wilson Allen, *Waldo Emerson: A Biography* (New York: Viking Press, 1981), p. ix.

3. Kenneth W. Cameron, *Ralph Waldo Emerson's Reading* (Raleigh: Thistle Press, 1941).

4. Allen, *Waldo Emerson,* p. 25.

5. Matthew Arnold, "Emerson," in Milton R. Konvitz, ed., *The Recognition of Ralph Waldo Emerson.* Selected Criticism since 1837. (Ann Arbor: University of Michigan Press, 1972), p. 73.

6. James Elliot Cabot, *A Memoir of Ralph Waldo Emerson* (2 vols.; Boston: Houghton Mifflin, 1887), 1:44.

7. Harold Bloom, *Figures of Capable Imagination* (New York: Seabury Press, 1976), p. 50.

8. Sherman Paul, *Emerson's Angle of Vision* (Cambridge, Mass.: Harvard University Press, 1952), p. 71.

9. Cf. *EL* 1:83 and *W* 1:15.

10. James Russell Lowell, "Emerson the Lecturer," in Konvitz, *Recognition,* p. 43.

11. William Wordsworth, "Written upon a Blank Leaf in 'The Compleat Angler,'" *The Poems,* edited by John O. Hayden (2 vols.; New Haven: Yale University Press, 1981), 2:398.

12. Page Stegner, *Escape into Aesthetics: The Art of Vladimir Nabokov* (New York: Dial Press, 1966), pp. 133–34 (italics his).

13. Paul, *Emerson's Angle of Vision,* p. 118.

14. Bliss Perry, "Emerson's Most Famous Speech," in Carl Bode, ed., *Ralph Waldo Emerson: A Profile* (New York: Hill and Wang, 1969), pp. 52–65.

15. Allen, *Waldo Emerson*, p. 431.

16. John D. McCormick, "Emerson's Theory of Human Greatness," *New England Quarterly* 26 (1953), 291.

17. Henry Nash Smith, "Emerson's Problem of Vocation," in Milton R. Konvitz and Stephen E. Whicher, eds., *Emerson: A Collection of Critical Essays* (Englewood Cliffs, N.J.: Prentice-Hall, 1962), p. 65, n. 20.

18. Ralph Waldo Emerson, "Reviews of Books," in *Uncollected Writings* (New York: Lamb Publishing Company, 1912), p. 140.

19. Many discussions of this issue are rather fatuous, but Perry Miller's essay, "Emersonian Genius and the American Democracy" (in Konvitz and Whicher, *Emerson*, pp. 72–84), is a brilliant exception.

20. Bloom, *Figures of Capable Imagination*, p. 63.

21. See the material collected in *W* 4:366–78.

22. Octavius Brooks Frothingham, *Transcendentalism in New England* (reprint ed.; New York: Harper Torchbooks, 1959), pp. 56–57.

23. McCormick, "Emerson's Theory," esp. pp. 293–96.

24. Rudolph Magnus, *Goethe as a Scientist*, trans. Heinz Norden (New York: Henry Schuman, 1949), p. 221.

Modern Science and Contemporary Discomfort: Metaphor and Reality

LEON N COOPER

I

Earlier in this series of lectures, Robert Penn Warren spoke on "The Use of the Past." One such is surely to situate the present. If for science the present seems unfriendly, we might, for comfort, recall the inscription on the dome of the great hall of the National Academy of Sciences in Washington:

TO SCIENCE
PILOT OF INDUSTRY
MULTIPLIER OF THE HARVEST
EXPLORER OF THE UNIVERSE
REVEALER OF NATURE'S LAWS
ETERNAL GUIDE TO TRUTH

The nineteenth-century optimist who wrote these words is, alas, no longer with us. Instead we have the professional demonstrator, the fundamentalist preacher, and the moralist legislator. Perhaps it is too much to say that we have fallen on the winter of our discontent.

But there are cold winds that blow from Washington, and the chill of indifference, even hostility, from the country as a whole, makes it somewhat unlikely that these words would be written today.

Possibly we have all become more sophisticated. We agree that science is useful, if a bit esoteric; scientists are not "with it"—like coiffeurs, fashion designers, or rock stars—nor are they as rich. There has been much noise about the evils of science and technology, but we know quite well that life as we have come to expect it would not be possible without the material fruits of science. And it is to science and technology that we look to solve such vast current problems as those of energy, disease, and poverty (also to solve the problems that result from the solutions), and to provide the means to ensure that the world's population does not simply increase to absorb the increased wealth that results from technological advances, leaving us with the same problems.

All of this appears to me to be more or less obvious. Yet when we are confronted by difficult practical judgments concerning science, an irrational element often dominates. This is an era characterized by skepticism about official pronouncements of any kind (a skepticism well earned, it is true, by official acts of the recent past). But beyond what one might call proper and reasonable distrust, in those discussions concerning the application of science to everyday affairs there lurks an uneasiness that is troubling enough to fuel the paranoia which seems so often to surface.

I suspect that this is so because even those who express respect for and admiration of science share, to some small extent, the feeling of science's bitterest critics. Writing recently in *Daedalus,* Theodore Roszak, not an admirer or a lover of science, invokes Mary Shelley, the child author of *Frankenstein, the Modern Prometheus:* "A girl of only nineteen . . . she joined the ranks of history's great myth makers. What else but a myth could tell the truth so shrewdly, capture definitively the full moral tension of this strange intellectual passion we call science? Asked to nominate a worthy successor to Victor Frankenstein's macabre brainchild, what should we choose from our contemporary inventory of terrors?" Roszak asks rhetorically. No lack of candidates: nuclear bombs, despot computers. "Modern science provides us with a surfeit of monsters, does it not?"[1]

However, he continues, "I have another monster in mind that troubles me as much as all the others—one who is nobody's child but the scientist's own and whose taming is no practical task. I mean an invisible demon who works by subtle poison, not upon the flesh and bone, but upon the spirit. I refer to the monster of meaninglessness. The psychic malaise. The existential void where modern man searches in vain for his soul." Further, he asserts that "it is science which has made our universe an unbounded theater of the absurd."

To most, this view will seem a trifle exaggerated. After all, Frankenstein monsters have been created by bureaucrats as well as by scientists, and the existential void may reflect personal as much as cosmic deficiencies. But this image of the Frankenstein monster is persistent and frightening. Are we afraid that science, like Victor Frankenstein, creates monsters, or—what is even worse—that science is itself the monster, destroying our values and our human worth?

There is a striking moment in the Mel Brooks film, *Young Frankenstein.* Near the conclusion of this farce, by a sequence of events too complex to detail here, the wordless and frightening monster suddenly speaks, and a remarkable transformation occurs. Though he is unchanged physically, the instant he speaks we are no longer afraid—as if with the utterance of words he ceases to inspire terror.

I think it may be that, for many people, science poses a threat that is perceived and felt, if not understood. Science is powerful and, like Mary Shelley's monster, moves with a directive of its own, oblivious to human value or desire. If there is an object to one more talk on this subject, it is to give words to this monster so that we might regard him without terror.

II

The monster that science is, opposed to those we create—the monster that has made our universe "an unbounded theater of the absurd"—arises more likely not from our material achievements, nor from what harm we have caused, but rather from the world view we have created (or those we have destroyed). Science has presented us with a truly remarkable vision of the world, a metaphoric view of reality that connects events from distant galaxies to living cells—of which we are justly proud. Let me remind you of some of these wonders: elementary particles and atoms, electricity and chemistry, DNA and living matter. We might conclude that what has not yet been explained we will be able to explain in the future, so that, as Victor Weisskopf has written, "man will eventually understand all of nature scientifically."

Yet it is just this vision that becomes a monster where

it shatters or makes difficult to retain other visions we want (or even need) to believe. Still, it is not correct to state that there is a single, timeless scientific view of the world; as science develops, its world view changes. Between the nineteenth and twentieth centuries, for example, we have gone through revolutionary changes due to the impact of Freud on psychology, Einstein on physics, and Darwin on biology.

Little was dearer to the nineteenth-century physicist than Newtonian mechanics and the wave theory of light. Yet, under the pressure of the new atomic phenomena, the assumptions underlying these theories were abandoned. Causality, a concept which underlies almost all of Western thinking, has been modified. David Hume had suggested that causality was not in the phenomena themselves but was a concept introduced to order our experience—the type of philosophical conjecture that elicits knowing smiles from working scientists. But to bring order to phenomena in the atomic domain, quantum theory—the twentieth-century replacement for Newtonian mechanics—has taken us from a completely deterministic theory to one in which equal causes do not produce equal effects. Einstein redefined time; the comfortable Swiss clock has been replaced in the popular imagination by a Dali grotesque. Possibly most threatening has been Darwin's great concept of evolution. Man, no longer the special—almost private—work of his Creator, has become but one link in an endless evolutionary chain.

Now these changes (even though they don't occur every day) are perfectly acceptable to scientists, but the change in world views they seem to imply does make some people nervous. Science poses for us, in a particularly acute form, a conflict between what we want to believe and what seems sensible to believe if one follows current fashion. For there are many beliefs that are dear to us, that we wish to retain—even though science does not need them to construct its theories.

A current example is the controversy concerning "special creation." It seems astonishing that such a debate should flare up again—an example of the tenacity with which some views are held. The claim is made that special creation is a valid scientific theory which should be given equal time with the conventional theory of evolution in the teaching of high school biology. This is so outrageous that it is hard to regard seriously. But such a claim does underline a general misunderstanding of what science is, and raises in a concrete form some interesting and serious questions: abstract questions, such as the relation between metaphor and reality, and very practical questions, such as who is to decide what a subject is and what we should teach in our schools.

One of the uses of the past is to remind us that all is not new. This is not the first time science has been told what it must believe and what it must teach. In a moving chapter ("The Starry Messenger" in the *Ascent of Man*), which some of you may have read, J. Bronowski writes of the confrontation between Galileo and the Church. In 1616 the Church ruled that certain propositions were to be forbidden:

> that the sun is immovable at the center of the heaven;
> that the earth is not at the center of the heaven, and is
> not immovable, but moves by a double motion.[2]

It has always astonished me that the Roman Church became so committed to a view of the universe that seems so peripheral to the central issues of Christian faith. (Previous errors don't seem to temper its strong views on current affairs today.) As is often so in human affairs, the path was complicated; in some ways it was almost an accident that the Ptolemaic view of the universe became Church doctrine.

When Aristotle was reintroduced into Europe via Latin translations of newly discovered Arabic translations of his notes, his views were regarded with a good deal of suspicion. There was a time, for example, when the teaching of Aristotelian physics was prohibited in Paris. However, through the monumental efforts of thirteenth-century scholars such as St. Thomas Aquinas (moved, I believe, in great part by their enormous respect for Aristotle's intellect), Aristotle's hitherto suspect views were "reconciled" with early Christian doctrine.

Although the reconciliation was never complete, from this time the Aristotelian conception of the universe became a part of the Christian drama of salvation. Thereafter, an attack on Aristotle became an attack on the Church itself. For such a variety of complicated reasons, by Galileo's time one view of a seemingly straightforward question about the world had become official Church doctrine. The issue was from then on political as much as scientific.

Galileo very likely made grave political blunders. We can imagine a revisionist historian earning his Ph.D. by casting him in the role of villain. Yet we are not profuse in our admiration of neighboring societies that make political issues of scientific questions (Soviet genetics or Nazi physics, for example). I think it must be a matter of eternal embarrassment that the holy Church went to the length of fabricating, and possibly forging, documents (so that, as you may have heard, the case has been reopened) to show Galileo guilty.

With the threat of torture, it wrung from this great man—seventy years old at the time—an abjuration of the heresy "of having held and believed that the sun is the center of the world and immovable, and that the earth is not the center and moves. . . ." "I abjure, curse and detest the aforesaid errors and heresies," Galileo swore.[3] But tradition, not willing to accept such ignominy, has it that under his breath he muttered, "Yet it still moves."

III

It is a common misconception that science is separated from the arts because science deals with fact or with information. As a critic puts it, "When the modern Prometheus searches for knowledge . . . he brings back . . . many candles of information," or "At one end (of our experience) we have the hard, bright lights of science; here we find information."[4] The scientist, as observer, is, of course, in some sense searching for the facts. I say "in some sense" because, in the absence of any theoretical préconception or organization, the so-called facts are close to meaningless. The full range of possible human experience is so large, the variety of ways of looking at the same events so diverse, that it is almost impossible to record our experience in any sensible way with no preconception as to what is significant. And, of course, these preconceptions often are the boldest strokes of organization.

Even if we could separate the mining of facts from the invention of theory, the view of science as information misses completely what seems to me is the most remarkable and, in a way, the most astonishing achievement of scientific thinking—that is, the creation of order, the organization of this so-called information. It is surprising that it can be done at all. As Einstein expressed it, "The most incomprehensible thing about nature is that it is comprehensible."

There is a sense in which the scientist, like the painter, poet, or novelist, is imposing an explicit ordering, created in his mind, on a more or less recalcitrant nature. The scientist's conception of the world is, of course, different in purpose and certainly different in detail from that of the poet. The ordering of Dante may seem imposed on reluctant reality, but in the perspective of today's quantum world, mightn't we regard the mechanistic Newtonian ordering, as seen by Laplace, for example, in the same way?

Having mentioned Dante, I can't resist showing you just one of Gustave Doré's illustrations of his remarkable journey, the ninth circle of Hell: three-faced Satan, frozen hip deep in a lake of ice, where, embedded for eternity to a depth appropriate to their crimes, are some of Earth's greatest sinners. On the right, if you look closely, you will see two figures: Dante and his personal guide, the Latin poet Virgil.

Dante was, of course, primarily interested in a moral order of the universe. But it is fascinating to observe how closely he followed the received astronomy and physics of his time. The center of Earth was the center of the Aristotelian universe, and it is the center (and the bottom) of Dante's as well: that point to which all

The Ninth Circle of Hell, by Gustave Doré.

heavy (sinful, earthy) matter is attracted. It is there that the creator of sin, Satan, is forever transfixed. Shortly, Dante and Virgil will begin their difficult climb down Satan's body (clinging to his hairy shanks), to descend to the very bottom of Hell (the center of the universe) and, having passed this point, begin the equally difficult ascent to Purgatory.

> From shag to shag he now went slowly down.
> Between the matted hair and crusts of ice.
> When we had reached that point just where the thigh
> Doth turn upon the thickness of the haunch.
> My leader, with fatigue and labored breath
> Brought 'round his head to where his legs had been,
> And grasped the hair like one who clambers up,
> So that I thought our way lay back to hell.[5]

In a Newtonian universe, their experience would have been more like that of an astronaut: they would have floated. (At the center of Earth, the gravitational force goes to zero.) This only reported experience seems to favor Aristotle.

For Dante, one senses that this invisible moral ordering of the universe is real: good rewarded, enshrined with the weightless and ethereal in God's empyrean; sin and evil fallen with the dross and heavy to the antipode, the center, their closeness to Satan determined by the weight of their sin—in strict correspondence with the physical universe as he believed it to be. It is as real as, and is what gives meaning to, daily experience of treachery, disease, and death.

And two millennia before Dante, in the First Book of Moses, called Genesis, the unknown poet wrote:

In the beginning God created the heaven and the earth. And the earth was without form and void; and darkness was upon the face of the deep. And the Spirit of God moved upon the face of the waters. . . .

Now it would seem that science is far removed from such metaphor—and in a sense it is. But when we ask what science means, the answer at any time may be regarded at least in part as metaphor. For though the structure of science often remains relatively unchanged, its view of the world changes radically. Is truth Newtonian determinism or quantum chance? Are these reality and literally true, or at least part metaphor? If part metaphor, how are they to be distinguished from poetic metaphor? How can we distinguish Newton from Dante, Darwin from Genesis? And which is to be called science?

IV

In their attempts to rebut "creationist" arguments, scientists and educators, perhaps in exasperation, have called creationism unscientific. A recent AAAS (American Association for the Advancement of Science) Resolution on Creationism resolves *"that because 'Creationist Science' has no scientific validity it should not be taught as science."* A recent article in *Physics Today* echoes this theme: "While theories in science are falsifiable, creationist beliefs are not."

There is a sense in which these statements are appropriate. If the creationist's view is that there was a single creation, it must account, among other things, for the fossil records—and these seem to indicate fairly unambiguously (as my colleague Kenneth R. Miller has pointed out) that there was either continual change or many separate creations. If the creationist's argument chooses to remain vague or confused on this point, it is not science, because it is not well defined (what is said does not depend unambiguously on what was said before).

However, it requires no great effort to construct a creationist argument that is well defined and is consistent with everything we observe: We need only assume that in the beginning God created the heaven and the earth and the fossil records.[6] (For that matter, we can assume that He created everything, including our memory of past events just before I began to speak.) The problem is not that the creationist view is unscientific, but that in any of its current variations it is not very interesting science.

But there is also a clear and major difference in motivation. Although science has from time to time maintained a world view (e.g., particles moving in a void as the basis for all experience), the view is second in importance to the precision of the assumptions, the logic of the structure, and its detailed correspondence with the "real world." As Galileo said, we must "make what is said depend on what is said before." His teachers of mathematics taught him this method. It is the elegance and naturalness of the hypothesis and the resulting structure that characterize what we call a beautiful theory. Science may present a vision of the world; but this scientific vision is the end result of a complex construction whose acceptance depends upon its detailed agreement with experience. The construction—the structure—has more permanence than its interpretation or meaning. This is evident, since from time to time (between the nineteenth and twentieth centuries, for example) the scientific world view has changed radically. Had we been led to the hypothesis that God created the world in six days and rested on the seventh, this would be our world view.

For the poet, it is richness of metaphor, ambiguity, and evocative quality of language that are of primary importance. He often begins with a world view, a moral order, a sense of the meaning of experience (in the case of Genesis, perhaps, an attempt to end a meandering, interminable dispute: Where do we come from? How did the world begin?), and searches for a means to express this view concretely. But whether Dante's vision is an accurate description of the world as it actually is or whether Genesis is a literal account of creation is almost completely irrelevant. The poetic message is clearly independent of literal truth or correspondence with the "real" world.

In contrast, for the creationist it is the world view that is a fundamental—in this case, the powerful metaphoric vision of Genesis. He shapes his hypothesis (if he is honest) or the facts (if he is not) to make the structure (such as it is) that evolves consistent with what he is willing to agree is observed, in such a way as to maintain the literal truth of his initial world view. His object is neither beauty nor power of expression, economy, and consistency of structure—nor even agreement with experience—but the preservation of his world view. His fundamental problem is not necessarily that he is incorrect or "unscientific," but that he had unfortunately converted magnificent metaphor into trivial science.

If the creationist argument can be made "scientific," how do we deal with the creationists' demand that they be afforded equal time in the schools to "answer" evolutionist arguments? This is non-trivial. For at heart are such questions as Who decides what science is? Who decides what is to be taught in our schools?

We note first that the so-called creationist theory is not a unique alternative to evolution. There are many creation myths. (In the first two chapters of Genesis there are two.) Which creation myth do we teach as an alternative to evolution? For every view taught in the schools there are hundreds of others—must we give all equal time?

The problem for the school system is whether it wishes to teach science or world views. If the choice is to teach science, a commonsense and conservative position would be that it is scientists who must determine what is good or bad science. We have found it sound practice to allow those in a profession to decide among themselves what the best opinions and practices of that profession are at any time. Clearly, the profession is not always correct (opinions, after all, change). But if the issue is how best to handle an airplane, how to do open-heart surgery, or what is a legitimate proof of a theorem, we generally let the pilots/engineers, surgeons, or mathematicians decide. Otherwise, we are faced with the spectacle of passionate orators arguing difficult and technical matters before audiences that do not have the competence to choose among the arguments. School children have the right to the best education possible. But it is not they who should decide highly technical differences between the experts.

Practical problems can arise: Are biologists so closed

to new or different views that rump groups must be set up to challenge them? Such a thing could happen. This is an empirical question and it would seem to me demonstrably false. I know many biologists. They display qualities common to the rest of us. Some are difficult, arrogant, or blunt; others are subtle, brilliant, and flexible. The profession as a whole is constantly debating new ideas. If "creation science" had any serious content, it would be debated just as earnestly as any of a dozen other ideas. What the community is telling us is that this so-called science is so bad or trivial it is not worth wasting time discussing. Yes, they might be wrong. But it is they who have to be convinced. If "special creation" is a scientific theory that can rival evolution, this must be argued before those who know the subject—not before school children.

Such arguments often have no logical resolution. Consider the following table, listing the ionic content of

Concentrations of Ions Inside and Outside Freshly Isolated Axons of Squid

Ion	Concentration (mM)		
	Axoplasm	Blood	Seawater
Potassium	400	20	10
Sodium	50	440	460
Chloride	40–150	560	540
Calcium	0.3×10^{-3}*	10	10

*The precise value of ionized intracellular calcium is not known. Data from Hodgkin (1964) and Baker, Hodgkin, and Ridgway (1971).

From Kuffler and Nicholls, *From Neuron to Brain* (Sunderland, Mass.: Sinauer Associates, 1976), p. 91.

axoplasm, blood, and seawater. I am led strongly to the conclusion that blood (largely seawater with red cells added for color) came into being when seawater was first employed by groups of swimming cells to provide a means for internal transportation of various goods and services—an argument, seemingly, for evolution. But, a counterargument might go, this is merely another manifestation of the economy practiced by an efficient Creator.

There is a lesson here for the teaching of science: science must be taught with the emphasis on logic and structure, rather than as a collection of "facts" that deliver the current scientific world view. When science is taught as a set of truths, rather than as a process of discovery, invention, and construction, we distort what science is and fall into a trap that makes us vulnerable to those with opposing world views.

V

It is the creationists' misfortune to have made their faith dependent on a literal interpretation of Genesis, thus running afoul of science—the supreme specialist in constructing a consistent ordering of the world that is. They are not the first to have maneuvered themselves into such an uncomfortable position. To defend their faith, they have made a bold and somewhat unconventional move: proclaiming themselves a science. By itself, this might be regarded as no more than an expression of desire—the triumph of desire over reason. Perhaps the desire is comprehensible. But the situation has become complicated by moralistic or opportunistic legislators who attempt to legislate desire as reality: to dictate what should be taught in our schools or to choose for us among various possible scientific hypotheses.

It requires a totalitarian mentality—or great naiveté—to legislate such things as the teaching of the creationist view, the moment of beginning of life, or even the value of π. One can legislate that $\pi = 3$ (as has been done), but that hardly changes the ratio between the circumference of a circle and its radius in a Euclidean space. (My own preference would be $2\pi = 1$.)

It is unnecessary confrontation. Science has discarded concepts such as those espoused by creationists—not, as might be suggested, because they are unscientific but because they are imprecise and uneconomical. The remarkable world view we have constructed does not require them.

Perhaps the most important result is psychological. Medieval man could live without embarrassment in a world whose reason, awareness, and concern were centered about him, just as the motion of the stars and that of matter, heavy or light, was centered about the Earth. It was a universe built around the drama of salvation, where, as in early Renaissance painting, all things had a purpose—an almost magical, luminous world where all of creation, from the angels to the beasts, and even inanimate stones, knew their place and their relation to everything else. He could believe, if he wished, that the words written in Genesis were literally true.

Possibly it is too much to say that modern science forces the abandonment of such a world, but its success makes one less comfortable living there. Justifiably or not, it is no longer easy to believe that the world has been constructed about man—that all of the creation, no longer centered about the earth, the result of the motion of particles subject to physical laws—is yet directed and ordered with man as the principal character in a grand drama. And that the Creator did his great work in six days, resting on the seventh.

And it is this, perhaps, that has led to some of the modern discomfort with science—not only among biblical fundamentalists but, more generally, as expressed by such critics as Roszak. Although it is not likely that science alone is responsible for the breakdown of the order we associate with former times (not troubling ourselves with such questions as whether this order was as benign as is suggested in retrospect—a winter scene of Breughel or the *Temptation of St. Anthony* of Hieronymus Bosch), although the breakdown of this perhaps sentimentally recalled ordered society is more likely a consequence of social changes (migration from the country to the city, industrialization, etc.), there was no doubt a contribution due to the increasing dominance of scientific thinking. And in the end the social fabric—not one thread only, but one thread after another—has been shredded, with little to replace what has been lost. Our disappointment is perhaps exacerbated by the ending of the nineteenth-century false hope that, somehow, scientifically generated values could replace those made increasingly untenable by the scientific world view.

A consequence for the twentieth century is a society that can perhaps be characterized as a "theater of the absurd," not in the cosmic sense but on a very individual level: a society in which there is no general faith or belief to guide action, in which the individual is often so separated from the important social consequences of his actions that individual social action seems meaningless, a society which seems plagued by what might be characterized as a generalized problem of the commons.

I do not believe, as is sometimes said, that "the average citizen" is incapable of rational, considered decisions; rather, we all have been placed in a situation in which such decisions (beneficial for the individual) are not beneficial for society as a whole. The "socially conscious" individual sees his attempt to behave in the common good mocked and vitiated, with statistical certainty, by the behavior of the others.

One often speaks of science's material services to man. But it is also possible that, as a greater service, we might eventually arrive at a world view which leads to a rationalization of the social situation. I don't mean at all an Orwellian world, but what is perhaps the opposite: a world the way Adam Smith hoped it would be, in which behavior is not regulated from above but, rather, as in a generalized marketplace, a world in which the individual can enjoy the consequences of clever and socially worthwhile behavior, a world in which the individual, acting rationally in his own interest, benefits society as a whole.

I realize that this may be asking too much of science or of scientists, since no doubt this is more than a purely scientific problem. It is a problem that can sometimes be attacked by appropriate taxation or financial incentives. But perhaps it is not too much to hope that our view of the world, which, no doubt, has contributed to the destruction of the "old faith," may some day contribute to a new rationalism in human affairs.

The early nineteenth-century scientific optimist is no longer with us. But I believe that the choice is not one between optimism and pessimism. One can as easily create scenarios with happy or unhappy endings. The choice, it seems to me, is between those who will try to agree on a path that can lead to success, and work to follow it, and those handwringers who can only point out the dangers and the risks that line any path and who will do nothing.

We can earn our place in the past, which we shall soon become, by creating the future. That, concludes Robert Penn Warren, "is the promise the past makes to us." In that promise there is no greater gift than our heritage of metaphor and structure—no greater burden than the heavy weight of outworn ideology.

Notes

1. Theodore Roszak, "The Monster and the Titan: Science, Knowledge and Gnosis," *Daedalus* (Summer 1974), pp. 17–32.

2. J. Bronowski, *The Ascent of Man* (Boston: Little, Brown, 1973), p. 207.

3. Ibid., p. 216.

4. In Roszak, "The Monster and the Titan."

5. Canto 34, *The Divine Comedy,* translated by Lawrence Grant White.

6. Such a view actually was presented in the nineteenth century by Philip Gosse in *Omphalos,* published in 1857. This was recently discussed by Stephen Jay Gould in *Natural History.*

Violence in American History: The Homestead Ethic and "No Duty to Retreat"

RICHARD MAXWELL BROWN

In topical terms, the variety of American violence has been enormous from the colonial period to the present.* We see criminal and outlaw activity, vigilantes, white mobs lynching blacks, KKK activity, family and community feuds, rebellious farmer-protest movements, land wars in the West, urban riots, religious, racial, and ethnic violence, industrial and labor violence, political violence and assassination, and, of course, homicidal individuals. There have also been peak periods of violence, such as the 1670s, '80s, '90s; the 1760s and '70s; the 1830s,

---

*When this slightly revised essay was delivered as a Franklin Lecture in May 1981, accelerating prices and interest rates were outgaining wages and salaries and making it more and more difficult for Americans to own their own homes. As this is being written in the summer of 1984 the rate of inflation has been sharply reduced, but interest rates remain high, and it is still very difficult for Americans—especially young Americans—to buy or build their own homes. A second condition of the spring of 1981 was a dramatic surge in violent crime. Since then the crime rate has gone down, but it is too early to know whether the decrease is part of a long-term downward trend or merely a temporary one. In any case, the incidence of violent crime is still very high and of the gravest concern to the citizenry.

'40s, and '50s; the 1880s and '90s; the 1910s, '30s, and '60s.[1]

In the last few years, there has been another significant upswing in American violence. The shooting of President Reagan certainly is an apt symbol for the surge in American violence that began in 1978. This current period began with a climb in the rate of violent crime and a succession of riots and political and racial murders. One of the earliest episodes was the late-1978 mass murder and suicide of over 800 members of the Jones colony in Guyana.[2]

Yet American violence, in its many guises and peak periods, has never been perpetrated by accident but has always been connected to major changes in the social, economic, and political factors of American life.

It seems that today our country is in another crisis period. The crisis, domestically, is twofold. First, the economic climate of inflation and unemployment, afflicting especially the northern and eastern United States, has produced a situation in which prices and interest rates outgain wages and salaries. Therefore, a depressed housing market is making it more and more difficult for Americans to own their own homes. Second, a dramatic surge in violent crime has made Americans more fearful of their lives and the sanctity of their homes than at any time, perhaps, in our history.

How will Americans respond to this twofold crisis, of threatened homes and threatened lives? Of course, it is too early to say for sure, but I contend that the public response will arise from a historical pattern of American behavior and American violence, exemplified by the two themes of the Homestead Ethic and "No Duty to Retreat." In this regard, let me point out that although we are now an urbanized nation, we have been, until rather recently, predominantly rural. Both the social doctrine of the Homestead Ethic and the legal doctrine of No Duty to Retreat are products of our seventeenth-, eighteenth-, and nineteenth-century past. Thus, I shall focus primarily on rural frontier violence in the main body of my remarks, before offering my concluding comments on the present crisis.

Before I discuss the American Dream of Success, I will present my concepts of the Homestead Ethic and No Duty to Retreat, which I will connect to a violent episode in late nineteenth-century California: the Mussel Slough conflict. This conflict illustrates the way in which certain rural Western Americans of the late nineteenth century reacted in their time, and it provides, I think, some lessons for our own time.

For the rural roots of our society and its violent tendencies, we must go back to the beginning—to the seventeenth and eighteenth centuries, when settlers from the British Isles were colonizing the Atlantic Coast. From those formative centuries of the American rural tradition emerged the Homestead Ethic, by which I mean the popular ethic of rural Americans from the eighteenth century to the twentieth—that is, a body of values on the basis of which, as the Homestead Ethic, rural Americans viewed life.

The very first colonists in New England adopted a practice that was unequaled in the Old Country: giving every adult male a free grant of land from the local town. This system was mirrored in the Middle and Southern colonies, where, under the head-right system, free grants of land of 50 or more acres amounted to a *de facto* homestead system for white farming families. By the time of the Revolution, rural Americans had grown deeply attached to the homestead, and the Homestead Ethic emerged as a cluster of values that dominated rural life. It formed an ideological basis for defense of the rural way of life.

Thus, there came to be four key elements in the Homestead Ethic: (1) belief in the right to have and to hold a family-size farm; (2) belief in the right to enjoy a homestead, unencumbered by a ruinous economic burden; (3) belief in the right peacefully to occupy the homestead, without fear of violence to family and property; and (4) belief in the moral premises associated with the homestead: work, thrift, piety, sobriety, and sexual morality.[3]

With the Homestead Ethic established by the middle of the eighteenth century, American farmers—especially of the back country and the West—often reacted violently then and later, when they perceived a threat to this ethic. Danger to the peaceful occupancy of land, emanating from the depredations of frontier outlaws, brought the response of vigilantism.[4] The self-defense reaction, based on the Homestead Ethic, was also triggered by Indian attacks and a cluster of economic problems—securing land titles against interlopers, trimming the burden of debt and taxation on small and medium-size farmers, and curbing land speculators. One tendency of rural life that also threatened this ethic was *social concentration*, a term used by historical demographers to label the process by which both land and wealth are increasingly concentrated in the hands of fewer and fewer well-to-do individuals.[5] This process endangered the Homestead Ethic twice: once in the middle and late eighteenth century, when back-country farmers found themselves in danger of losing their land, which caused a wave of nine rebellious movements that were largely successful.[6] The second surge of social concentration, in the late nineteenth century, also engendered a wave of violent rural action in defense of the Homestead Ethic. (Of this, I shall have more to say in a bit.) In short, I maintain that a transition from Old Country attitudes to the American Homestead Ethic is a key to the emergence of much rural violence in the eighteenth, nineteenth, and twentieth centuries.

A second transition from Old Country values parallels the rise of the Homestead Ethic and is also a key to rural American violence. This transition relates to a change in our legal doctrine which is, however, both an outgrowth and a part of the experience of rural frontier life. I am referring to the emergence of the American legal doctrine of "stand one's ground"—that is, there is no legal duty to retreat in the face of an aggressive enemy. This relates indirectly to the Homestead Ethic, but directly to individual violence in rural American life—to the connection between individual violence and the historically violence-prone character of rural Americans. Thus, in the combat-prone history of the frontier West, the epitome was the violence of individual against individual in the gun duel, or "walk down": two men walking toward each other in a dusty Western street, ready to draw, fire, and kill. The walk-down is closely linked to what John Cawelti has called the "six-gun mystique" of the West,[7] and is embedded in the myth of the West through such novels as *The Virginian* (by Owen Wister) and such classic movies as *High Noon*.[8]

But the walk-down is not merely part of the myth of the West, it was part of the reality as well. As a gun duelist, no one exceeded the fatal skill of John Wesley Hardin of Texas,[9] but the tradition of the walk-down seems to have been initiated by Wild Bill Hickok, the so-called Prince of Pistoleers, shortly after the Civil War in the southwestern Missouri town of Springfield. Toward sundown of a hot July day, rural Missourians were milling about the town square of Springfield in anticipation of violence between Hickok and one Dave Tutt. It was well known that there was bad feeling between the two, and as the shadows lengthened, Hickok and Tutt started pacing across the square toward each other. They opened fire at virtually the same time, but Hickok was the better shot, and he survived this prototypical Western walk-down whereas Tutt did not. Hickok's exploit was given national publicity, and he went on to a spectacular career as a gunslinger in the Kansas cowtown of Abilene and elsewhere.[10]

It is true that the walk-down did not occur with the frequency that it does in fiction and film, but it occurred often enough to become part of the Western tradition. Aside from its frequency, the walk-down has had enormous significance in one aspect of rural, frontier, Western violence: the irreducible factor of violence in homicide.

In connection with homicide as an aspect of rural violence, I want to show how the frontier experience had a crucial impact on the American system of legal values and how those values (as always) reflected the broader system of American values. At issue here is how the common law in England and America has dealt with those who have been tried for homicide in courts of law. In England, ordinarily, a person who committed a homicide was tried for and convicted of murder, unless he could prove that he had acted in self-defense—in which case the court would find his homicide justifiable and he would therefore be found not guilty.

Thus, traditional English common law as imported to America by the colonists had *no permissive* provision for or attitude to homicide in self-defense.[11] Under English common law, one could successfully plead justifiable homicide only if one could prove that he had obeyed the common-law *duty to retreat* (that was the legal phrase, "duty to retreat") before killing in self-defense. Under this doctrine, one's first responsibility was to *escape* from the scene altogether, to flee, in which case *no* killing could occur. There were situations in which escape from a man bent on doing harm was impossible, yet even in such dire cases the common law, down to the time of Coke and Blackstone, did not allow one, without penalty, to *stand and fight* and, if necessary, kill one's assailant in self-defense. Instead, the law held that one was obligated to retreat as far as possible—"to the wall at one's back" was the legal phrase—and only when the wall was reached would the law allow one to turn and kill one's assailant to avoid being killed.[12] The thrust of the English common-law doctrine, therefore, defused homicidal situations by causing the self-defender to flee altogether—or to retreat to the wall at his back. More broadly, the object of this common-law doctrine was to lessen the instances in which disputes would be settled by personal violence. To the individual victim of aggression, the common law said in effect: You must get away—not defend yourself, not settle the dispute yourself—but later, if you wish, you may take your opponent to court and allow the government, through its court, to settle the dispute. (The duty to retreat sounds strange to American ears, but in my opinion it is one reason why the English homicide rate has been notably lower than ours.)

In the United States during the nineteenth century, and under the impact of the frontier experience, the common law pertaining to homicide was Americanized and the English legal duty to retreat was replaced with a new, typically American legal doctrine: no one had the duty to retreat. Instead, you could stand your ground and fight back, and legally kill in self-defense, without first retreating. Also, the necessity to flee was abandoned. In state after state during the middle of the nineteenth century, supreme courts, in upholding the stand-one's-ground doctrine, proclaimed that the duty to retreat was inappropriate to American conditions. In effect, these courts held that to flee or retreat from a homicidal situation was a cowardly act, in keeping with neither the American character nor American conditions.

There was a rural, frontier factor in all of this. By 1900 the duty-to-retreat doctrine was enforced in very few states, chiefly in the oldest-settled areas of the Eastern third of the United States. It was in states west of the Appalachian Mountains, with their rural, frontier heritages, that key judicial decisions had been handed down—decisions which replaced the legal duty to retreat with the legal right to stand one's ground. State supreme courts in Ohio, Indiana, Minnesota, Missouri, and states farther West, obliterated the duty to retreat; and in one Southwestern state, Texas, to stand one's ground was put into the penal code as well as the common law. Indeed, the no-duty-to-retreat doctrine became strongest of all in the society and law of Texas.[13]

The triumph of the rural/frontier doctrine of standing one's ground and the negation of the duty to retreat were embodied in an opinion by the Supreme Court's most accomplished legal philosopher and phrasemaker, Justice Oliver Wendell Holmes, in the 1921 case of *Brown* v. *United States* (Brown was no relation to me). Aptly enough, the Brown case came out of Texas, where, in a dispute between two construction workers, Mr. Brown had killed Mr. Hermes. The two men had been on the outs, and their festering hostility came to a climax on the job, when Hermes came at Brown with a knife and Brown stood his ground and killed Hermes with a gun. Since the homicide was on federal property—a post-office construction site—the case was heard in a federal court. Although there was no duty to retreat under Texas law, this point had not yet been settled in federal case law. In the lower federal court, Brown was convicted of murder because he had not obeyed the English common-law duty to retreat. He appealed, and his case was heard by the U.S. Supreme Court, which reversed the conviction and held that Brown *did* have a right to stand his ground. In his opinion for the majority, Justice Holmes wrote approvingly of the stand-one's-ground doctrine, and in one telling phrase summed up the whole trend of U.S. society and history and the Americanization of the common law of homicide when he wrote that there is no duty to retreat in the face of "an uplifted knife."[14]

In general terms, the shift in American legal values which replaced the duty to retreat with the right to stand one's ground was similar to the shift in social values which, in the frontier West, came to view the killing of one's opponent in a walk-down as brave and honorable. Thus the walk-down and its related attitude to homicide, no duty to retreat, became not just part of the code of the West but of the American code of behavior.[15] The spirit of the new legal doctrine of stand-one's-ground and contempt for the idea of retreat were summed up in the folk wisdom of the refrain of an old Smoky Mountains ballad: "I ain't no hand for trouble, but I'll die before I'll run."[16]

Abolition of the duty to retreat in favor of stand-one's-ground helps us understand the emergence of a rural American society in which combat was not only highly approved but often expected. It helps us understand how on May 11, 1880, two groups of rural Californians squared off against each other in a sun-drenched wheatfield. Although not a walk-down in the technical sense, the implacability with which each group faced the other resembled a walk-down in its psychology. In a matter of minutes, guns were discharged and six persons were dead—until that time, the largest number in a face-to-face gunfight between white civilians in Western history (many more than were killed one year later in the famous gunfight at the O.K. Corral in Tombstone, Arizona, in which the Earp brothers and Doc Holliday took part).[17]

The gunfight of May 1880 was the climactic violent episode in what has come to be known as the Mussel Slough conflict. But before I amplify the details, however, I want to put it in historical context, involving the Homestead Ethic and social concentration. In the period 1865 to 1900, social concentration was behind the great land wars that wracked the West, by which wealthy and powerful individuals and corporations attempted either to push pioneers off the land or make them pay dearly for occupancy.[18] The famous Johnson County War in 1892, in which the Wyoming Cattlemen's Association used violence to exclude small ranchers and homesteaders from the ranges, was a pattern of conflict that appeared often in Texas, Oregon, Nebraska, Montana, New Mexico, and many other parts of the West.[19]

Another kind of conflict in this period, also related to land in the West, was between the railroads, which had obtained grants of millions of acres from the federal government, and the settlers who wished to occupy that land. Such a conflict, which epitomized the alignment of elite wealth and power against pioneer settlers of small means, was the Mussel Slough conflict in California in the 1870s and 1880s, between wheat farmers who had turned Central Valley desert land south of Fresno into a veritable garden by toilsome and expensive irrigation and, having done so, saw the Southern Pacific Railroad, headed by the "Big Three"—Collis P. Huntington, Leland Stanford, and Charles Crocker— claim these now lush lands under the terms of a federal land grant.[20] To the pioneer farmers of Mussel Slough, the Southern Pacific Railroad was attempting to monopolize the land of honest, hard-working yeomen.

The center of the Mussel Slough country was the small town of Hanford, which in 1880 was only three years old. Today, Hanford is a community of about 15,000 and one of the liveliest cities of the Central Valley, and the Mussel Slough country is one of the most beautiful garden spots of California, whose small and medium-sized farms are dotted by stately and graceful orchards and vineyards and watered by gushing irrigation ditches, dug by the original homesteaders. One can visit the field where, more than a century ago, six men suffered death wounds, and one can still see the live oak—the "tragedy oak," as it came to be known—within sight and sound of the shooting.

Hundreds of Mussel Slough pioneers joined the Settlers' Land League to defend their homesteads against the Southern Pacific. Court records show that the typical Mussel Slough settler occupied about 130 to 160 acres, and typical of these struggling settlers was Robert B. Huey, who was born in Pennsylvania but had been a Californian since 1856. He married in 1865, took a hand at school teaching, and then moved to a quarter section (160 acres) of Mussel Slough in 1869. With a growing family, Huey built a house, dug a well, and planted shade trees and a garden, but did not do well on the near-desert land until, in 1872, he began irrigating it with Kings River water from a big canal that was dug and maintained by Huey and his neighbors. Irrigation enabled Huey to plant almost all his land in grain, and he prospered well enough to build a barn, plant an orchard and vineyards, and make an addition to his house. Then, in 1878, the blow fell. Attorneys of the Southern Pacific Railroad sued Huey for possession of the 160 acres that he had improved (to the extent of $3500 in labor and capital).[21] Like many other settlers, Huey claimed the 160 acres under the preemption land law of the U.S. government, but the railroad claimed the land as part of its huge federal grant in the 1860s.

Huey and hundreds of others, as I've noted, had joined the Settlers' Land League of Mussel Slough farmers and, with such leaders as Thomas Jefferson McQuiddy and John J. Doyle, refused to knuckle under. They held that the railroad had failed to live up to the terms of the congressional grant and, therefore, the controverted land remained in the possession of the federal government and was open for preemption, as in the case of Robert B. Huey. In a petition to President Rutherford B. Hayes in 1880, Huey and 254 other settlers invoked the Homestead Ethic to bolster their claim:

> We organized irrigation companies and saturated the sterile plain to the extent of hundreds of thousands of acres. We accomplished this work in the face of great natural obstacles with very little means and under extreme conditions of hardship, toil, and endurance. Through sheer energy and perseverance and by the investment of our means through the best years of our lives and relying firmly upon our rights as American citizens and upon the pledges of fair treatment by the Southern Pacific Railroad we converted a desert into one of the garden spots of the state. We secured fairly and honorably permanent homes for ourselves and our families and we erected school houses and churches, laid out roads, and supported thriving villages, and one considerable town. . . . We founded an American community in which peace and order, honesty and decency, industry and economy, plenty and comfort prevailed.[22]

The railroad magnates, of course, had *their* side of the story. Huntington, Stanford, and Crocker felt their claim to the land was good, and that their enterprising activity was responsible for building California and developing the West. The three men had their own ethic—the capitalistic property owners' ethic—by which they justified their actions.[23] It was a classic American situation, in which each side genuinely thought it was in the right.

Thus, by 1880, the Mussel Slough country was a tinder box on the point of explosion. The irate settlers held that the railroad, in effect, violated point one of the Homestead Ethic: the right to a family-size farm. So they adopted the vigilante spirit, following California frontier precedent, when they organized as "night riders" to attack, harass, and intimidate supporters of the railroad. They vowed not to give up their land without a fight.[24]

On the other hand, two supporters of the railroad, Mills Hartt and Walter J. Crow, went about armed to the teeth, practiced target shooting, and referred to the settlers as "sand-lappers," a California equivalent of the term "redneck." The more dangerous of the two was Crow, son of an old California pioneer. He was known as the best wingshot in California, and Ambrose Bierce was later to salute Crow's "terrible courage" and refer to him as the "bravest of Americans."[25]

Both sides were spoiling for a fight, and it soon came. In the spring of 1880, the railroad moved forward with its lawsuits to dispossess the farmers, or make them pay up. Thus, on the pleasant morning of May 11, 1880, a heavily armed party of four, headed by the U.S. marshal and including the railroad's local land agent and the implacable violence-prone Hartt and Crow, set forth across the Mussel Slough wheatfields to eject two settlers and to install Hartt and Crow in their places.

One ejectment was perfunctory, because the occupant was away at a settlers' picnic, and his possessions were simply thrown out of his house and onto the roadside. As the railroad party rode on in buggies to carry out its second dispossession, it was confronted in a wheatfield, near a huge live-oak tree, by forty or fifty Settlers' League members. Although the foursome was in buggies and the settlers were on horses, both sides stepped to the ground, and the psychology of the confrontation was much like that of a walk-down. Tense words escalated to an argument and a sudden burst of gunfire, as a settler named Harris and Mills Hartt exchanged shots. Hartt's gun spoke an instant before Harris's shot mortally wounded Hartt. In retaliation, Crow sprayed the settlers with bursts from his breech-loading shotgun. Harris was killed with a shot in the chest; then in rapid succession, four other settlers were slain or fatally injured by Crow. With Crow's last shot, the firing stopped, for by then the only armed settlers were dead or dying. Crow escaped but was caught in a field, a mile and a half away, by a band of settlers who shot him dead.[26]

As a violent climax to the farmers' attempt to defend their homesteads against the Southern Pacific Railroad's land-enclosing tactics, the May 11 shootout—as the news flashed over telegraph wires to the state and the nation at large—had a strong impact on public opinion. To many Americans in May 1880, the event seemed to represent the height of corporate heartlessness and greed. The "lesson" of the deaths of seven men—five of whom were farmers who had opposed the railroad—seemed to be that one of the greatest American corporations, the Southern Pacific Railroad, headed by three of the most powerful and wealthy men in the nation, was not content to deprive hard-working farmers and family men of their homes but would demand the ultimate sacrifice and have them shot in cold blood.[27]

Although the Mussel Slough shootout of 1880 is almost forgotten today, it gripped the emotions of Americans in the late nineteenth century. Forty-four thousand Californians signed a petition to President Hayes in support of the farmers and against the railroad,[28] and one of America's greatest intellects, the young California-born Harvard philosopher, Josiah Royce, wrote and published (1887) a novel based on the Mussel Slough tragedy.[29] Indeed, novelists were intrigued by the human dimension and the play of economic forces in the shootout. In all, five novels have been based on the bloody doings of May 11, 1880—the best and best-known of which is the powerful American classic *The Octopus* by Frank Norris, published in 1901 and still in print.[30]

The homesteading wheat farmers, who had opposed the Southern Pacific with guns at Mussel Slough and with legal briefs in courts of law, ultimately lost. The federal circuit court in San Francisco, presided over by a judge who was a close friend of Stanford and Crocker, ruled adversely on the settlers' claims, and by the late 1880s the majority of them were gone—dispossessed by the legal action of the railroad.[31]

Let me repeat: by the late 1880s the majority of the Mussel Slough farmers were gone. This brings me to a point I mentioned at the outset, which I want to develop: rural American violence must be connected not only to the factor of land (as I have done in stressing the

Homestead Ethic) but also to the decline of rural life—to the mass movement of rural Americans to the city, especially from 1865 to 1970.

In a gripping book on rural violence, *Wisconsin Death Trip,* the historian Michael Lesy, writing about rural Wisconsin in the 1890s, depicts the traumatic events that caused farmers and townspeople to move to the big city in large numbers.[32] In so doing, Americans were exercising the option of mobility and turning their backs on the problems of rural life—leaving behind numbing drudgery, threats of social concentration and land monopoly, the explosive violence represented by the Mussel Slough conflict—and moving to the city for, they hoped, something better.[33]

In other words, rural Americans of the late nineteenth century had at least two options in coping with problems such as those the Mussel Slough settlers faced. One option was violence, for which the traditions of the Homestead Ethic and no-duty-to-retreat had prepared them. Another option was mobility: simply give up on rural life, go to the city, and start over.

Mobility has long been recognized as a key factor in American life, but the recent research of social historians is giving it a new meaning and clarity. The new research on mobility is helping to solve one of the key problems in understanding American history, and that is the persistence of the American Dream of Success,[34] of upward social mobility—the idea that by hard work and thrift an American can rise from the lower class to the middle class or from the middle class to the upper class.[35] Some scholars would say that the American Dream is a fraud, because research has shown that, by and large, upward social mobility has not occurred and that most Americans, no matter how hard they have worked and saved, remain in the social class into which they were born. But if this is the case—and it *is* the case—why have Americans always believed in, and why do they continue to believe in, the American Dream of Success? The answer is found in considering geographic mobility in contrast to social mobility. Geographic mobility is sometimes called "horizontal mobility," to indicate that when a person moves geographically, that person changes residence but not class.

We have always known that Americans moved around a lot, but in recent years abundant research has shown just how remarkably mobile Americans have been.[36] The key statistical index of this geographic mobility is the turnover rate, which shows how many inhabitants are left in a given community after a lapse of ten years. Research has shown that in the nineteenth century, in a typical Eastern city, 50 to 60 percent of the population had moved after only ten years and was replaced by a growing number of mobile newcomers, many of them immigrants from Europe. In the rural/frontier communities of the Midwest and West, the turnover rate was much, much higher, with only about one quarter remaining in a particular community after the passage of ten years.[37]

Thus, the departure of the Mussel Slough settlers, after they were forced off the land by the railroad, was in keeping with the broader trend of geographic mobility and the even broader trend of the decline of rural American life. The option of violence—standing one's ground in defense of the homestead, as did the five farmer-martyrs who died in the Mussel Slough wheat-field on May 11, 1880—was an option that failed. What about the other option, geographic mobility?

In my research on the Mussel Slough conflict, I have followed the later career of one of the leading settlers, who, after the failure of violence and legal resistance, exercised, like the other settlers, the option of geographic mobility. The man in this case was John J. Doyle (whom I mentioned as a major leader of the settlers), whose career reveals the new tack of individual enterprise after the failure of violent group action. In Mussel Slough, Doyle had grown wheat on a tract whose title he disputed with the railroad. He did well as a farmer, and he became the spark plug in the farmers' legal campaign to defend their homesteads against the railroad. An activist to the core, he lobbied Congress in the late 1870s in behalf of the Mussel Slough settlers, and he masterminded the unsuccessful legal campaign. While Doyle was heading the legal effort, his violence-prone colleagues in the Settlers' League engaged in anti-railroad night riding. Doyle did not take part in the May 11 shootout, but he served a term in a U.S. jail for conspiracy to oppose the U.S. marshal, and one interpretation holds that Doyle was the mastermind of the violent activity, as well as the legal campaign, of the Settlers' League.[38]

But by the late 1880s, Doyle was a defeated man. Mobility was forced upon him when he lost his land, and he took his family into the Sierra Nevada Mountains, 50 miles east of the Mussel Slough country. Soon, he and his family were living in a huge redwood log, hollowed out to make two rooms.[39] Doyle was down, and almost out, but irrepressible, and he still dreamed the American Dream. Ultimately, he became prosperous in the booming, open, mobile society that was California between 1890 and 1910, for he had made an about-face. Instead of opposing land operators (like the railroad), he became a land developer and speculator—not on a huge scale, but large enough to gain economic success for himself and his family. In this departure, Doyle diverted the boundless energy he had used against the railroad into a new cause, for he had seen the resort potential of the beautiful mountain country where he and his family lived (in a log). He acquired U.S. government land, for which at first there was little demand, then sold it off—125 lots in all—at a healthy profit to people who wanted to build summer homes in the mountains in the cool, clear heights above the hot, dusty Central Valley.[40]

With the gains from his imaginative and successful promotion, Doyle returned to the Central Valley in the early 1890s. He avoided the Mussel Slough country, with its searing memories, and went to the bustling little city of Porterville, where he became a leader in real estate sales and promotion.[41] John J. Doyle had thus been successful in making the transition from farm to city life, but he did not change his class status. As both a Mussel Slough farmer and a Porterville realtor, he remained a member of the middle class. There was no upward social mobility, but Doyle prospered in Porterville. The American Dream of Success was fulfilled in modest prosperity in the urban phase of his life.

The case of John J. Doyle is typical, for the researches of social historians have established that the vitality of the American Dream is perpetuated not by upward mobility but by improvement within one's class. Satisfaction came to factory workers who labored hard and saved enough to buy their own homes. These homes were not grandiose, nor did the workers rise above their class, but the emotional lift from owning one's home was like that of the farmer who owns his home-stead.[42] The same sort of thing occurs when the salary or wage earner, who remains all his life in an urban blue- or white-collar job, comes to possess his own home, buys a better car (and maybe a boat), and sends his children to college. For him, the American Dream of Success is validated.

And here I return to the Homestead Ethic, as I offer my concluding theme: Both the values and the violent tendency of rural America have been perpetuated in the now predominantly urban environment of Americans. We must not forget that many Americans, over the twentieth century, were first- or second-generation rural people in their social origins.[43] They have brought with them to the city the cultural heritage of the countryside, and this heritage has focused on the Homestead Ethic. This ethic lives on in our time, in the sense that although the farm or ranch or small town has long since been left behind, the goal of the urban era remains closely tied to the Homestead Ethic, in the form of homeownership. For most urban Americans, ownership of a home, whether in the central city or suburbia, has come to mean fulfillment of the American Dream.

However, the American dream of success for those of middle- and lower-class status is threatened—especially in the North and East—as it never has been before. Today, the impact of inflation is analogous to that of social concentration in the eighteenth and nineteenth centuries. The result is that a socially dangerous gap may open between the extremely well to do, on the one hand, and those of medium and lesser means on the other hand.

Not long ago, both of America's leading news-magazines, *Time* and *Newsweek,* published long cover stories on the surge of violent crime that is menacing city, suburb, and countryside.[44] In our crime-beleaguered nation, there is another analogy to the rural frontier and back country of the nineteenth century. In my view, public reaction to these conditions is shaped by, and will draw upon, the historical heritage of the Homestead Ethic and No Duty to Retreat.

The economic impact of inflation, with its accelerating costs and sky-high interest rates, by making it more difficult (often impossible) for Americans to acquire homes and keep them, threatens the American Dream of Success and violates the first tenet of the updated Homestead Ethic: belief in the right to a family-size home of one's own. Moreover, the surge of violent crime violates another tenet of the updated Homestead Ethic: belief in the right to occupy a home peacefully without fear of violence to family and property. This, likewise, is a threat to the American Dream.

It is too early to say exactly how Americans will respond to these two dangers to the modernized, up-dated Homestead Ethic, but so deeply has our past embedded the ethic in our national heritage that the response, I am confident, will be powerful. In this connection, the continuing vitality of No Duty to Retreat is evident, for all authorities are in agreement that civilians are arming themselves at a rate unequaled here-tofore in this century. The commitment to self-defense in behalf of the individual and the family as embodied in the belief in No Duty to Retreat, is sweeping the nation, as *Time* and *Newsweek* show. The confrontation between the aggressive, crime-prone element and those who are motivated by the defensive concepts of the Homestead Ethic and No Duty to Retreat may become the most explosive in America's long history of violence.

Notes

1. Richard Maxwell Brown, *Strain of Violence: Historical Studies of American Violence and Vigilantism* (New York: Oxford University Press, 1975), chap. 1.

2. Among many studies of the Jonestown episode, see James Reston, Jr., *Our Father Who Art in Hell: The Life and Death of Jim Jones* (New York: Times Books, 1981).

3. Richard Maxwell Brown, "Back Country Rebellions and the Homestead Ethic in America" (pp. 76–79), in Brown and Don E. Fehrenbacher, eds., *Tradition, Conflict, and Modernization: Perspectives on the American Revolution* (New York: Academic Press, 1977). See also David P. Handlin, *The American Home: Architecture and Society, 1815–1915* (Boston: Little, Brown, 1979).

4. Brown, *Strain of Violence*, chaps. 4–6.

5. Kenneth A. Lockridge, "Social Change and the Meaning of the American Revolution," *Journal of Social History* 6 (1972–73), 403–39.

6. Brown, "Back Country Rebellions."

7. John G. Cawelti, *The Six-Gun Mystique* (Bowling Green, Ohio: Bowling Green University Popular Press, 1975).

8. Owen Wister, *The Virginian* (New York: Macmillan, 1902); *High Noon* (1952), directed by Fred Zinneman.

9. Lewis Nordyke, *John Wesley Hardin: Texas Gunman* (New York: Devin-Adair, 1957).

10. Joseph G. Rosa, *They Called Him Wild Bill: The Life and Adventures of James Butler Hickok* (Norman: University of Oklahoma Press, 1964); Kent Ladd Steckmesser, *The Western*

Hero in History and Legend (Norman: University of Oklahoma Press, 1965), chaps. 10–15.

11. Roy Moreland, *The Law of Homicide* (Indianapolis: Bobbs-Merrill, 1972), pp. 259–61.

12. Ibid., pp. 261–68. Frederic and Joan Baum, *Law of Self-Defense* (Dobbs Ferry, N.Y.: Oceana, 1970), p. 6.

13. Francis Wharton, *The Law of Homicide*, 3rd edition, ed. Frank H. Bowlby (Rochester: Lawyers' Cooperative, 1907), p. 355. Among important state supreme court decisions, see *Erwin* v. *State*, 29 Ohio St. 186 (1876), and *Runyan* v. *State*, 57 Ind. 80, 84 (1877). Three studies which deal with the demise in the United States of the legal duty to retreat are *Columbia Law Review* 41 (1941), 733ff., and *Kentucky Law Journal* 20 (1932), 362ff., and 39 (1951), 353ff. On Texas, see G. W. Stumberg, "Defense of Person and Property under Texas Criminal Law," *Texas Law Review* 21 (1943), 17, 32; Henry P. Lundsgaarde, *Murder in Space City: A Cultural Analysis of Houston Homicide Patterns* (New York: Oxford University Press, 1977), pp. 145, 164; and Brown, *Strain of Violence*, chap. 8.

14. *Brown* v. *United States*, 256 U.S. 335 (1921). Mr. Justice Harlan's opinion in favor of stand-one's-ground, in *Beard* v. *United States*, 158 U.S. 550 (1895), had not been definitive.

15. For example, President Dwight Eisenhower, in a speech on November 23, 1953, paid tribute to Wild Bill Hickok, the spirit of the walk-down, and, in effect, the stand-one's-ground doctrine. Steckmesser, *Western Hero*, p. 158, n. 16.

16. Epigraph to C. L. Sonnichsen, *I'll Die Before I'll Run: The Story of the Great Feuds of Texas* (New York: Devin-Adair, 1962).

17. On the O. K. Corral, see Bill O'Neal, *Encyclopedia of Western Gunfighters* (Norman: University of Oklahoma Press, 1979), pp. 102–3.

18. No one was more alert to the issue of land monopoly in California and the West, and its contradiction of the

Homestead Ethic, than Henry George in the following writings (volume and page numbers are for his *Complete Works* [10 vols.; New York: Doubleday, Page, 1906–1911]): *Our Land and Land Policy* (1871), 8:5, 20, 33–38, 49, 52, 68–69, 71–72, 94–95, 99; *The American Republic . . .* (1877), 8:168, 171; *Progress and Poverty* (1880), 1:389; *The Land Question* (1881), 3:74–75; and *Social Problems* (1883), 2:21–23, 232.

19. The prototypical treatment is by Helena Huntington Smith on the Johnson County War: *The War on Powder River* (New York: McGraw-Hill, 1966). Filled with needless historical distortions, Michael Cimino's powerful though flawed film, *Heaven's Gate* (1981), nonetheless catches the spirit of the Johnson County War, on which it is based.

20. The following discussion of the Mussel Slough conflict and John J. Doyle is based upon research for my book in progress on the conflict. Space does not permit me to cite all of the many, many primary and secondary sources of my research.

21. Case No. 2037, *Southern Pacific Railroad Company* v. *Robert B. Huey*, in Old Circuit Court (1865–1911) case file, Federal Archives and Records Center, San Bruno, California.

22. A microfilm copy of the petition, with its signatures, is in the Bancroft Library of the University of California at Berkeley (call no.: Film/C-A/ 2170).

23. Collis P. Huntington to F. H. Gassaway, October 22, 1894 (Huntington Family Papers in the Huntington Library, San Marino, California), expresses and defends the ideology of development by capitalistic enterprise, a theme that is given scholarly expression in Richard J. Orsi, "*The Octopus* Reconsidered: The Southern Pacific and Agricultural Modernization in California, 1865–1915," *California Historical Quarterly* 54 (1975), 197–220.

24. *Visalia Weekly Delta,* November 29, 1878, p. 2, c. 3, and July 25, 1879, p. 3, c. 6 (Visalia was the county seat of Tulare County, in which the Mussel Slough conflict took place); *History of Tulare County, California* (San Francisco: W. W.

Elliot, 1883), pp. 195–97; James L. Brown, *The Mussel Slough Tragedy* (n.p., 1958), pp. 140–47.

25. Irving McKee, "Notable Memorials to Mussel Slough," *Pacific Historical Review* 17 (1948), 21; interview with Frank Latta, Santa Cruz, California, August 11, 1978; Ambrose Bierce, *The Wasp* (San Francisco, 1881), p. 293.

26. The preceding account of the shootout is based on eyewitness descriptions by parties on both sides, in *Visalia Weekly Delta*, May 14, 1880, p. 3, c. 1–5, and May 21, p. 3, c. 1–3.

27. *Visalia Weekly Delta*, May 21, 1880, p. 2, c. 2, and May 28, p. 2, c. 5; *Harper's New Monthly Magazine*, November 1882, pp. 874–75; McKee, "Notable Memorials," p. 19.

28. *Visalia Weekly Delta*, March 4, 1881, p. 4, c. 4; Eugene L. Menefee and Fred A. Dodge, *History of Tulare and Kings Counties* (Los Angeles: Historic Record Co., 1913), p. 112.

29. Josiah Royce, *The Feud of Oakfield Creek* (Boston: Houghton, Mifflin, 1887).

30. Frank Norris, *The Octopus: A Story of California* (New York: Doubleday, Page, 1901). The three other novels are William C. Morrow, *Blood-Money* (San Francisco: F. J. Walker, 1882); Charles C. Post, *Driven from Sea to Sea; or Just a Campin'* (Chicago: J. E. Downey, 1884); and May Merrill Miller, *First the Blade* (New York: Knopf, 1938).

31. The judge was Lorenzo Sawyer (*Dictionary of American Biography*, s.v.), whose decision against one settler (*Southern Pacific Railroad Company* v. *Pierpont Orton*, case no. 2035, in the case files cited in note 21, above) was simply repeated in dozens of surviving anti-settler decisions (case nos. 2036–37, 2160–65, 2282, 2317, 2320–22, 2358, 2361–2479).

32. Michael Lesy, *Wisconsin Death Trip* (New York: Pantheon, 1973).

33. Much of our most vivid writing of the late nineteenth and early twentieth centuries is a literature of despair. Such writers as Edgar Lee Masters, Ellen Glasgow, Hamlin Garland, Sherwood Anderson, Sinclair Lewis, and William Faulkner portray the bitter and depressing life that induced

Americans by the millions to flee from the countryside to the apparently brighter horizons and greater possibilities of the city.

34. Anthony Brandt, in "Now and Then: The American Dream" (*American Heritage* [April–May 1981], pp. 24–25), credits James Truslow Adams' 1931 book, *The Epic of America* (Boston: Little, Brown), with coining the phrase.

35. Among the scholars who have dealt with the American Dream of Success is W. Lloyd Werner, *Structure of American Life* (Edinburgh: University Press, 1952), chap. 4; and the following works stress the success ideology: John G. Cawelti, *Apostles of the Self-Made Man* (Chicago: University of Chicago Press, 1965); Richard M. Huber, *The American Idea of Success* (New York: McGraw-Hill, 1971); Kenneth S. Lynn, *The Dream of Success: A Study of the Modern American Imagination* (Boston: Little, Brown, 1955); Donald Meyer, *The Positive Thinkers* (Garden City, N.Y.: Doubleday, 1965); Moses Rischin, ed., *The American Gospel of Success: Individualism and Beyond* (Chicago: Quadrangle, 1965); Richard Weiss, *The American Myth of Success: From Horatio Alger to Norman Vincent Peale* (New York: Basic Books, 1969). Kevin Starr, *Americans and the California Dream, 1850–1915* (New York: Oxford University Press, 1973), illuminates the California version of the American Dream.

36. This trend of research, now well advanced, was initiated by Stephan Thernstrom's first book, *Poverty and Progress: Social Mobility in a Nineteenth Century City* (Cambridge, Mass.: Harvard University Press, 1964), a work whose title, significantly, reverses Henry George's title, *Progress and Poverty.*

37. Don Harrison Doyle, "Social Theory and New Communities in Nineteenth-Century America," *Western Historical Quarterly* 8 (1979), 155.

38. Menefee and Dodge, *Tulare and Kings Counties,* pp. 801–2.

39. Floyd L. Otter, *The Men of Mammoth Forest . . .* (Ann Arbor: Edwards Brothers, 1963), pp. 101–2.

40. Ibid., pp. 35, 51, 91–92, 101–2, 104; Thomas H.

Thompson, *Official Historical Atlas of Tulare County* (Tulare: n.p., 1892), pp. 70, 104.

41. Menefee and Dodge, *Tulare and Kings Counties*, pp. 801–2; Otter, *Men of Mammoth Forest*, pp. 101–2.

42. Thernstrom, *Poverty and Progress*, pp. 117–37. See also Handlin, *American Home*, pp. 352, 356, 370–77.

43. Handlin, *American Home*, chap. 2 and *passim*, focuses on house and home in dealing with the transition from the rural America of farm and small town to the urban America of the twentieth century.

44. "The Curse of Violent Crime," *Time*, March 23, 1981, pp. 16–33; "The Plague of Violent Crime," *Newsweek*, March 23, 1981, pp. 46–54. For background in scholarly depth on the recent surge of crime, see Charles E. Silberman, *Criminal Violence, Criminal Justice* (New York: Random House, 1978).

U. S. Grant:

The Man in the Memoirs

JAMES M. COX

Since my larger subject is autobiography and my particular subject is U. S. Grant, let me begin with a touch of personal autobiography. Here at Auburn in the Deep South I can only hope that my Southern accent can be at least faintly heard, for I am from the South—the "Upper South," I suppose I should say. Virginia is my native state, but I was not born just anywhere in Virginia. My home is in southwest Virginia, in the mountains. The farm on which I was raised—I use the word advisedly—is 2,800 feet above the sea, a higher elevation than any farm I know of in New England, where I have taught for twenty years. So I think it might be better to say I am from the High South—though from the perspective of the Deep South it might seem more like the Shallow South. Politically, it was certainly "shallow" at the time of the Civil War.

Every true Virginian cannot forget that western Virginia went with the North when the war began and was made a state as part of the political effort to add free states to the Union by injecting strong political leverage into the military force that was accumulated to change the Constitution. And even in the mountainous part of southwest Virginia, western North Carolina, eastern Kentucky, and east Tennessee there was great sympathy with the North. Even so, my people went with the South. My grandfather was a captain in the Confederate Army and was wounded in the battle of Gauley Bridge early in the war; he was brought home along 200 miles of rutted roads for a semi-paraplegic life that lasted until 1903. I say "semi-paraplegic" with a certain emphasis, because he married and had eleven children.

I cite these facts not as credentials but perhaps as an explanation for my long-standing interest in the Civil War. There was not, as I remember, much talk in my home about that war. My mother, who had come from Pulaski County, just to the east of my native Grayson County, could remember her uncles—one of whom had fought with Lee, the other with Joseph E. Johnston—arguing over the merits of those two commanders. My father knew, and knew well, the broad outlines of the struggle, but rarely stressed the Civil War as a subject of conversation. Yet somehow I was more interested in the war than any of my schoolmates were. I can remember reading Mary Johnston's *The Long Roll* and Clifford Dowdey's *The Bugles Blow No More* early in high school, and then going beyond fiction to read Douglas Southall Freeman's four-volume biography of R. E. Lee. And I can never forget what for me was the strongest passage in Faulkner's *Intruder in the Dust*, because, reading it at the University of Michigan just after returning there from World War II, it seemed to sound some depth of my emotional life. The passage is part of Chick Mallison's remembrance of his uncle Gavin's voice, speaking for him the truth it no less seemed for me:

It's all *now* you see. Yesterday won't be over until to-morrow and tomorrow began ten thousand years ago. For every Southern boy fourteen years old, not once but whenever he wants it, there is the instant when it's still not yet two oclock on that July afternoon in 1863, the brigades are in position behind the rail fence, the guns are laid and ready in the woods and the furled flags are already loosened to break out and Pickett him-self with his long oiled ringlets and his hat in one hand probably and his sword in the other looking up the hill waiting for Longstreet to give the word and it's all in the balance, it hasn't happened yet, it hasn't even begun yet, it not only hasn't begun yet but there is still time for it not to begin against that position and those circum-stances which made more men than Garnett and Kem-per and Armstead and Wilcox look grave yet it's going to begin, we all know that, we have come too far with too much at stake and that moment doesn't need even a fourteen-year-old boy to think *This time. Maybe this time* with all this much to lose, and all this much to gain: Pennsylvania, Maryland, the world, the golden dome of Washington itself to crown with desperate and unbelievable victory the desperate gamble, the cast made two years ago; or to anyone who ever sailed even a skiff under a quilt sail, the moment in 1492 when somebody thought *This is it*: the absolute edge of no return, to turn back now and make home or sail irre-vocably on and either find land or plunge over the world's roaring rim.[1]

I have always liked the fate in my life that took me North to read that passage, just as I now like the fate that has brought me South to speak of U. S. Grant—a hard figure to face, even for an American, let alone a Southerner. Both Southerners and Northerners saw him as a killer during the Civil War; even worse, remembering that he had grown up the son of a tanner, they saw him as a butcher. At Shiloh and in the assaults before Vicksburg, he had shown how prepared he was to endure large losses of men. And in the Wilderness and again at Spotsylvania, he sustained losses in direct confrontation with Lee that no prior commander could stand without retreating. Finally, at Cold Harbor, when he lost 7,000 men in a little over eight minutes, Northerners as well as Southerners, though they could see that he would never turn back, had to wonder whether anyone on either side could endure the arithmetic of such a victory.

In the 120-year aftermath of that struggle, the nation has tended to see him as the stubborn and relentless figure who plunged from Shiloh to Appomattox, seemingly careless of the cost in lives, "to fight it out on this line if it takes all summer."[2] Lincoln and Lee, the other two men who live in the national memory as the central triumvirate, have been largely exempted from responsibility in the slaughter. Lincoln's martyrdom and Lee's surrender have left them with an increasingly benign image. Yet we have to know, if we have read Shelby Foote's magnificent narrative of the Civil War, that it was Lincoln who, long before the Wilderness, had realized that what the Northern army required— what *he* required—was a general who could withstand such arithmetic.[3] Moreover, it is well to remember that Grant tells us, in his *Memoirs*, that about the only subject in which he was good at West Point was mathematics.[4] As for Lee, his gentle face in all those portraits obscures the fact that he was as much a killer as Grant. From the moment he took command of the Confederate forces in the Seven Days east of Richmond, he showed a disposition to attack—and often to attack entrenched positions. Thus if Grant's strategy at Shiloh and at Chickasaw Bluffs prefigured the Wilderness and Cold Harbor, Lee at Malvern Hill prefigured Pickett's charge at Gettysburg. To think about Lincoln and Lee and Grant this way, it seems to me, is to begin to comprehend how prepared they were to bear the responsibility of killing in the war. Bearing that kind of killing was what McClellan and his Confederate counterpart, Joseph E. Johnston—both of whom were profoundly loved by their men—couldn't quite endure. They lacked that ultimate willingness to give battle.

Looking at the war with hindsight, as we must, we see the fatality of Grant ultimately facing Lee—and where but in the *Wilderness*, only 15 miles wide and 8 miles deep, and not in the West, or in the mountains, but in the East, only 50 miles from Washington. It is as if that term *wilderness*, so integral to anything we could think about America, were to be contracted, confined, and concentrated into an arena where two men—one from the South and East, from a great American family related by blood and marriage to the immortal Washington, and groomed to lead a ragged army of revolution, not altogether unlike the one that Washington led; the other from the North and West, from obscure stock and an even deeper obscurity into which he had withdrawn, or sunk, to emerge into prominence through a series of victories at Donelson, Shiloh, Vicksburg, and Chattanooga—were to face each other as battle-tested representatives of their societies. The fierceness of that encounter still has power to exhilarate, but also makes us tremble, no matter where our sympathies lie. The savagery of attack made Grant, who whittled while the battle raged, tremble in his tent afterward[5]—but did not deter him from his purpose, as Lee's ferocity had shattered Hooker and Pope and Burnside. Grant tells us that his army cheered when he pointed it south toward Spotsylvania instead of north across the Rappahannock (as his predecessors Hooker and Burnside had done after their initiation under Bobby Lee's fire),[6] but there is no record of its cheering after Cold Harbor. Yet—cheering or not—Grant's army kept up such pressure in effort after effort to flank Lee's army that Lee, his maneuverability increasingly lost, had to submit to the siege of Petersburg. Though he fought brilliantly, and exacted a horrible toll, he could never regain the offensive against the man who, his soldiers said, "didn't scare worth a damn."

At Appomattox, although Lee said that he would rather die a thousand deaths than surrender, he nonetheless surrendered—precisely to avoid the thousands of deaths that *he* could not die. The fine thing about his surrender was that it was unconditional; thus it was not abject. Grant laid down the conditions, and they were generous. If it seems one of the noblest moments in American history, it is because both men were noble in the moment. For Lee, the poignance was the loss itself; but there was poignance as well in Grant's generosity—for he gave away his nobility. He could never be so noble again. Yet he did not throw it away; he *gave* it away. Left with that nobility—his own, coupled with that which Grant had obscurely granted him—Lee rode away from Appomattox on Traveller, the wonderful horse with the wonderful name. The road of his career went not to the presidency of his nation, as that of his model, Washington, had gone, but to the presidency of a ravaged and all but ruined Washington College in Lexington, Virginia. Though he thought of writing about the war, he did not. He lacked the records and, more important, he lacked the life. The war, which had been his life, was truly over. What was left was not to be a life of writing but of silence on the subject, a composure of submission, humility, duty, and above all simplicity—a model so restrained and severe as to be a monument of education for the life of defeated young men returning into a victorious Union. And so Lee, like Lincoln before him, died into immortality—idealized in the South and forgiven in the North, as Lincoln was idealized in the North and more and more forgiven by the South. Of the three, Grant alone realized the full material benefits of victory and went on to be President of his nation, only to find in that success a wilderness of failure, until at last, in the throes of bankruptcy and the sickness that would kill him—cancer of the throat (no doubt brought on by all the cigars he smoked)—he wrote his memoirs.

All this is prologue to consideration of those memoirs and the man in them who is my subject. But memoirs, as much as war, are both a form and act of life. Walter Benjamin, in an essay on the writer Nickolai Leskov, has some fine observations about the nature of a man writing at the point of death. He observes that after World War I the very idea of narration or storytelling had declined.

With the [First] World War a process began to become apparent which has not halted since then. Was it not noticeable at the end of the war that men returned grown silent—not richer, but poorer in communicable experience? What ten years later was poured out in the flood of war books was anything but experience that goes from mouth to mouth. And there was nothing remarkable about that. For never has experience been contradicted more thoroughly than strategic experience by tactical warfare, economic experience by inflation, bodily experience by mechanical warfare, moral experience by those in power. A generation that had gone to school on a horse-drawn streetcar now stood under the open sky in a countryside in which nothing remained unchanged but the clouds, and beneath these clouds, in a field of force of destructive torrents and explosions, was the tiny, fragile human body.[7]

Later in the essay, Benjamin points out how death, which had once been the source of man's authority, is steadily sequestered from the living in sanatoria or hospitals—and today, we could add, in nursing homes.

It is, however, characteristic that not only a man's knowledge or wisdom, but above all his real life—and this is the stuff that stories are made of—first assumes transmissible form at the moment of his death. Just as a sequence of images is set in motion inside a man as his life comes to an end—unfolding the views of himself under which he has encountered himself without being aware of it—suddenly in his expressions and looks the unforgettable emerges and imparts to everything that concerned him that authority which even the poorest wretch in dying possesses for the living around him. This authority is at the very source of the story.[8]

To be sure, Benjamin is thinking in terms of story and fiction, rather than autobiography, but his remarks on what the First World War did to narrative—or rather on the relation between the emotional devastation wrought in that war and the disappearance of narrative in the modern world—might well be applied to our Civil War. Gertrude Stein was surely right in seeing that America, far from being the world's newest nation, was actually the oldest, for the precise reason that in its Civil War it was the first nation to enter the modern world. It is not merely that the Civil War marked the introduction of mechanized war on the grand scale, that it heralded vast troop movements by railroads, that it signaled the beginning of aerial observation by means of balloons, that it ushered in the rifled guns and breech-loading carbines, that it marked the appearance of iron-clads, harbor mines, and submarines in naval warfare, that it initiated fully developed trench warfare, that it introduced the telegraph as the common means of communication, and that it perfected mass killing to the point of institutionalizing the body count. Beyond all these innovations, the war was the most wholly *written* war that had ever occurred. Not only were official records written by officers after each engagement—and ultimately published in 128 volumes by the U.S. government—but reporters were constantly in the field, covering the war.

For example, Charles A. Dana of the New York *Tribune* accompanied Grant on numerous occasions. And illustrators like Winslow Homer and Alfred Waud were on hand. In addition, there were the photographers, of whom Brady is merely the best known. He not only waited in Washington for famous people to come to him, he also went into the field in search of them; thus he was in Richmond to photograph Lee three days after Appomattox, before the light of battle in his eyes had faded. The ten-volume photographic history of the Civil War, published in 1910, in addition to being the first photographic war history of such scope, remains a classic. And of course there were the memoirs—hordes of them—by prominent officers as well as soldiers in the ranks.

Today, we are likely to think that memoirs are autobiography, since they are so classed in libraries. But the term *autobiography* is of relatively recent origin; there was no such word until the end of the eighteenth century. Thus what is today called Benjamin Franklin's *autobiography* was called by Franklin *memoirs*, indicating that it was an account of his public or external life. The term used for a chronicle of one's inner life was, following St. Augustine, *confession*. Yet the emerging term, *autobiography*, had, by the end of the nineteenth century, so completely carried the field that it came to stand for both the inner and outer lives of personal narrative. Significantly, the term first appeared when *self* was displacing *soul* as the term to designate the individual life—the same historical moment when the American and French revolutions, freeing the individual as a potent political energy, established nations which, more and more separated from God, were themselves to become a religion. In our own national life, the Civil War signals that moment when the religious sensibility, already cast adrift in the constitutional separation of church from state, was violently attracted from the church into the political arena. Thus Lincoln himself seems always to be a kind of Christ figure as President, and his death on an April Friday in 1865 is connected in our minds to that other Friday that we can't quite separate ourselves from. His Emancipation Proclamation, rededicating Jefferson's Declaration in the cadences of church rhetoric, stands in the American mind as the primary document of our national religion.

Grant, however, was not Lincoln. He called the account of his life a memoir, not an autobiography, and he remains, on the whole, stolidly secular in that account. Yet his *Memoirs* are not exclusively about his public life, beginning as they do with his early "private" life, pursuing his life as a soldier first in the Mexican War and then on his Civil War campaigns, and concluding with a chapter defining what he believes that war meant in the life of his nation. Insofar as his book begins at the beginning of his life and follows his rise from obscurity into prominence, it is an autobiography; insofar as it refuses to deal extensively or intensively with his inner life, it is a memoir (in the old sense of the term). It is clear almost from the beginning, and remains clear to the end, that Grant saw his life in terms of his military and not his political career. Thus his memoirs are in effect military memoirs and, as such, they relate him to Caesar and Napoleon. Although Napoleon did not live to publish his memoirs, on St. Helena he dictated much of his life to four members of his staff (Bertrand, Las Cases, Gourgaud, and de Montholon). Like Caesar, he spoke of himself in the third person, knowing that this usage at once related him to the preeminent military figure of the classic world and reflected his imperial identity as a separate force in history.

Grant does not, of course, speak of himself in the third person. He was, in the first place, not an emperor, but a general and president. Moreover, he was an

American, and he wanted to remain a simple separate self, to use Whitman's formulation, and at the same time be a representative of the American possibility in the manner of Franklin, rising from obscurity to prominence. There is, for all the inevitability of that first-person pronominal *I* to designate the self, a severe problem for anyone who writes about himself in the first person. Although everyone uses the pronoun in the confident assurance that it refers to the ineffable and singular self, there remains the relentless fact of language, all but forcing everyone to resort to the self-same signifier. If we are writing about our inner, emotional selves—if, let us say, we are truly unknown and are attempting, in the act of writing, to make ourselves known, whether to ourselves or to an intimate or impersonal audience—then we have to intensify our individuality by dramatizing or lyricizing or explaining our lives in such a way as to inscribe by the very act of writing our lives imperishably upon the page, lives which, but for that very act of writing, would remain unrecorded and unknown. Thus the very life itself, in such a case, depends on the writing. If such an act of writing puts immense pressure on the writer to secure his signature in autobiographical discourse, he nonetheless enjoys the freedom of his material, since there is no large referential record against which his writing can be tested.

With a writer like Grant, the situation is vastly different. His life had taken shape publicly; indeed, his life by the time he came to write it had already been *written* by history. And so he already had a vast record to deal with. Though that record had made him known and interesting, thus ensuring an audience for what would seem to be at last *the* authentic record of a life, the outlines and substance of which were widely known, he nonetheless faced a profound problem. Beyond making good his own account—setting the record straight, introducing material that only he could know, marshaling his evidence into coherent sequential narrative—Grant, if he were truly to succeed, had to repossess or reclaim his life from history. Otherwise, why write it? Why not, like Lee, somehow assent to history in the faith that the life, as existing in the public and historic records, would itself be the deed of gift to posterity?

The moment we come to the motive of writing one's own life, we all but touch the heart of autobiography. I do not wish, in probing the sources of the form, to slight the baser motives in such writing acts, particularly the acts of famous people. We can see, in the memoirs of Eisenhower, Truman, Nixon, and Carter, the strong commercial motive—so strong that it usually ensures failure in the very marketplace it is too much designed for. And certainly the commercial motive was as strong in Grant as in any of the recent presidential memoirists I have named. He had, as William McFeely has emphasized in his fine biography, come to the idea of writing his memoirs as a means of financially recovering from the questionable and disastrous speculative investments he had made—investments sufficiently disastrous and questionable to tarnish, if not taint, his already damaged reputation.[9] Indeed, the only way Grant could avoid the taint was to maintain an innocence so profound as to make him seem almost stupid. If the innocence shielded him from culpability in the political and financial world he had entered after Appomattox, it seemed all the more to expose his naked desire for power and money.

Grant was of course fortunate in having Mark Twain as his publisher, not only because he got the most liberal terms of royalty any writer could expect but also because in Mark Twain he encountered a writer equally interested in the commerce of authorship. It was Mark Twain, after all, who had written to Olivia Langdon Clemens that he wouldn't touch a subject "if there wasn't money in it." Much as genteel writers and later academic critics might deplore the outright mendacity of such an author, few could deny that Mark Twain was every inch a writer. Beyond that, Grant had found in Mark Twain a kindred spirit—a Westerner who, in the world of writing, had determined to command a vast audience in much the same way that Grant had commanded a mighty army. After hearing Mark Twain lecture in Boston, William Dean Howells observed that he had held his audience in the palm of his hand and tickled it. Then too, Mark Twain, who had felt the full sting leveled at him by literary Boston after his irreverent performance at the Whittier birthday dinner in 1877, was already making the myth of himself as the Confederate soldier who, having had the sagacity to resign—as he humorously referred to his desertion—from the Confederate army in 1861, because Grant was pursuing him in Missouri, nonetheless had the power of humor to reduce his erstwhile nemesis to helpless laughter at the reunion of the Grand Army of the Republic in Chicago in 1879. At that reunion, where speaker after speaker toasted the celebrities on the platform—Grant, Sherman, Sheridan and others—Mark Twain had watched the imperturbably deadpan Grant sitting unmoved, with one leg across the other, while speaker upon speaker shook the house with eloquence. As the last speaker, Mark Twain chose as his subject "the babies," and observed that it was humbling to think that all people, even the heroic Grant, had once been babies. He went on to imagine Grant in his cradle, fifty-six years earlier, utterly devoted to the immensely serious strategy of trying to get his big toe in his mouth, and he ended by claiming that few in the audience could doubt that he had succeeded. I have always thought that the humor of the remark had much to do with Grant's posture on the platform—the head possibly leaning forward toward the one leg across the other, in profound concentration on the foot. In any event, the toast, which had the same irreverent audacity of the Whittier fiasco, and no doubt produced in the assembled throng a corresponding anxiety as Mark Twain worked through those drawling pauses in leading up to his snapper, brought the house down, and Grant with it—at least in Twain's triumphant account to Howells.[10] There was, no doubt, something particularly gratifying for Mark Twain in recounting his success to Howells. Like Grant, who had also come from Ohio, Howells had sufficiently succeeded in the genteel literary community of Boston to show undue embarrassment in the wake of the Whittier affair.

If Clemens, as Confederate veteran, had enjoyed his triumph over Grant upon the Chicago stage, he enjoyed even more his role of rescuing him from the menace of bankruptcy—and rescuing him in the role of *publisher*, thereby making Grant a writer under Mark Twain's protection rather than the general who had menaced him in the distant past. To see such possibilities is not at all to demean the relationship between the two, but to begin to appreciate it. It was, after all, a happy and productive relationship, and had a happy conclusion, at least in the financial sense. The Webster Publishing Company, of which Twain was senior partner, paid Julia Dent Grant a single royalty check of $200,000, the largest such check in the nineteenth century.[11] And so Grant's last sustained act of life left his heirs fully solvent.

So much for the financial motive. If that motive seems negative in terms of what we like to think of as *literary* purpose, it is at least irrelevant in terms of the literary value of the book—though we can say that Mark Twain's faith in the commercial value of the *Memoirs* prompted him to see that the book was produced in handsome style. There are, however, other negative motives that bear upon a critical valuation of the book itself. There is always a suspicion on the part of a sophisticated reader about an autobiographer's willingness or ability to tell the truth of his life. Hence the belief that either vanity, fear, repression, or downright suppression of evidence will disable the autobiographer, making his account unreliable. That is why we wait for the biographer to give us the "real" truth of the life. Nor can we exempt Grant's account from such a charge.

He makes no mention of mutely accepting the registrar's error at West Point that changed his name from Hiram Ulysses Grant to Ulysses Simpson Grant, surely one of the crucial facts of his life. Nor does he tell about his drinking, an accusation that was brought against him throughout his career. When after Vicksburg, he went on a binge, riding hell for leather through and over tents and campfires on a horse named Kangaroo, you may be sure that he does not regale us with that episode in his *Memoirs*. Nor does he tell of the drinking he must have done in San Francisco before the war, when, apparently in despair in the loneliness of being far from home at a military outpost in a country of speculators, gamblers, and derelicts, he may have felt doomed to join the failures who were the casualties of a society dreaming of striking it rich. To know those hidden "facts" is to want to read between the lines of Grant's steadfast, prosaic account of this losing campaign in the Far West that led him to resign from the army, and led to further defeats as a farmer, as a candidate for public office in St. Louis, and finally to total retreat into his brother's leather goods store in Galena, Illinois (not far from Hannibal, Missouri, where Samuel Clemens had gotten his start, and on the same great river where the same Samuel Clemens was even then a pilot). Nor is there any mention of the night after the battle of the Wilderness, when Grant threw himself so violently on his tent cot that Horace Porter could never forget it.

Then, too, there are distortions. On the matter of Shiloh, Grant is singularly circumspect in accounting for the surprise attack he faced from Albert Sidney Johnston, though it is possible to see through the circumspection to something having gone awry on that first day of the battle. And at Iuka, Grant puts heavy stress on the way the wind blew the noise of battle away from him—in order to explain his failure to know that a battle was being fought in the vicinity of his responsibility. And in describing the Chattanooga campaign, Grant evades the fact that Sherman, his favorite commander, was held in check by Pat Cleburne, while Thomas, for whom Grant had carefully engineered a subordinate role, took Missionary Ridge. Indeed, anyone who wished to explore just how Grant *always* depreciates Thomas might have a field day of research.

Could it be that Grant, ever eager to promote himself and his favorites, Sherman and Sheridan, might have been concerned, to the point of anxiety, about Thomas' having come so grandly to the fore in the eyes of the nation after his brilliant action at Chickamauga? To the very end of the *Memoirs*, Grant consistently depreciates Thomas on grounds that he delayed giving battle, and he can do little more than grudgingly acknowledge the completeness with which Thomas finally routed Hood's army. As for Bobby Lee, Grant is hardly magnanimous prior to his account of Appomattox. A reader of the *Memoirs* would do well to check Freeman's *R. E. Lee* as a corrective to Grant's version of all the battles leading to the Confederate surrender, though a reader of Freeman would be equally bereft of an objective view of that year-long campaign if he hadn't read Grant's *Memoirs* with extreme care. And a reader of Grant, K. P. Williams, Bruce Catton, Allan Nevins, and even Shelby Foote's masterful and definitive narrative of the war is left with Lee's profound silence on the subject—a silence that grows all the more powerful the deeper one plunges into the memoirs of Longstreet, Hood, E. P. Alexander, Jubal Early, Sherman, Horace Porter, and Sheridan—to touch but the surface of this sea of narratives.

To insist on Grant's self-protection, or whatever one wishes to call it, may seem to some a disparagement of his account. How far that is from my intention I can hardly say. I simply wish that I was deep enough into this subject to point to a hundred more examples of such evasion, or even self-serving, by way of launching an initial attack on Grant that would bring fully to the fore the solidity, the stubborn, straight-ahead narrative with which Grant completed his life. Though the *Memoirs* may seem to those who contemplate Grant's life from the biographical perspective the partial life it so surely is, for me it is the complete, which is to say the essential, life of U. S. Grant. And I have no doubt that the biographical subtext, no matter how much it is completed down the years, until the last of a thousand discrepancies is shown between it and Grant's text, will but all the more validate the authority of the *Memoirs*.

What is that authority that I see and foresee? First of all, it comes from Grant's having reclaimed authority over his life by the act of authorship. Never mind that even his authorship *was* contested soon after the appearance of the *Memoirs*, contentions having been made that either Adam Badeau or Mark Twain ghosted the book. One has but to look at the work of Badeau, a skillful writer, or that of Mark Twain, a great and inimitable writer, to see the folly of such claims. The point is that Grant, in the presence of death, and writing almost to the point of death itself, literally completed his life. In that sense he "took" his life, for there is always a suicidal impulse in the act of autobiography, whether the writer knows it or not. If he writes well, he ends his life. It is no wonder that Henry Adams, writing to Henry James after completing his *Education* (in which he had converted himself into the third person), advised James to take his own life before a biographer had the chance to take it.

To begin to see the task that faced Grant in writing his

life—beyond the sheer act of will required to execute his life before death executed him—one has to imagine the difficulties and complications surrounding him. First of all, as I have said, his life had already been written, and more than that, his campaigns had already been criticized by other memoirists. He himself had joined the fray of conflicting accounts in *Battles and Leaders of the Civil War*, published by *Century* magazine. So there he was, faced by the remorseless enemy, Death, that he knew was waiting directly ahead of him, and flanked by conflicting accounts of leading participants in the war—some of praise, others of blame, some Union and some Confederate—all claiming the authority of experience. Then, too, there was the essential failure of the success of his life after Appomattox, which led him to squander not only the ample remuneration that he had been given by a grateful nation but also the honor he had so justly won. All this and so much more constituted the remorseless divisions of the enemy. For Grant, like every true military figure, not only had enemies, he *required* them.

Now how to write his way directly into this conflict, without complaining about the enemy and without getting committed to justifying himself? There was the problem, sufficient to tax the ablest writer. There would have been every enticement to evade it by being fulsome in praise of others or overmodest in evaluation of himself, as a means of disarming both friends and foes. And think for a moment of a much larger invitation—to simplify, in an utterly false way, by reducing the topography of this battle into smooth terrain, as if the battle of the writer were not a wilderness of contradictions into which the very current of narrative had to run and, somehow, run through—as Grant's life had run, all but unconsciously forward, its great ambition not so much concealed as coordinated and literally embodied in the disarming figure of the man who walked as if he were slightly pitched forward.

The more conscious Grant was about these divisions of the enemy, the more likely he was to do what other memoirists did: explain, justify, complain, insist, brag, sentimentalize, and reveal. Yet to have no explanation, no justification, no criticism, no sentiment, no morality, no pride, and no revelation was indeed to have nothing. And you may be sure that in the *Memoirs* there is explanation, justification, criticism of the most telling kind, sentiment, moral vision, calm pride of achievement, and a great deal of revelation. But the point is that all these aspects of mental existence are subordinated to the command of a forward-moving narrative.

That narrative is—and the point seems to me crucial—much more conventional than original in conception. Even so, the convention, which begins with the lineal descent of parentage on both sides of the family, eventuating in the birth of the subject, has already divided Grant into the two "I's" that constitute every first-person autobiography. There is the generating "I" of the writer, all but concealed to the reader, and the conceived "I," who seems to the reader, and even to the writer, submerged in the convention, the subject of the book, though that "I" is really the object for the writer—the object being drawn along the utterly conventional line of chronology to the present consciousness generating it. Now the generating consciousness of the writer can try to be at one with what it believes to have been the emotions of the past self, or it can be detached and extremely objective about that past self. Grant's narrative runs conventionally between these extremes.

The past self that Grant presents in his narrative, which is to say the boy and young man with which his book begins, is also profoundly conventional. He is, in other words, primarily a *general* boy and young man. This does not mean that he is ordinary, nor does it mean that no particular life is presented. There are fine details. There is the boy who loves horses—yet the love is never presented poetically, or what we might want to call "imaginatively." Horse is a horse is a horse, as Gertrude Stein would say (who, incidentally, wrote acutely about U. S. Grant). But horses are present all through Grant's *Memoirs*, and that presence is a kind of solid and pervasive fact about the life of the man in his book. Here, it is nice to remember that almost the only time Lee waxed poetic in his letters is about the incomparable Traveller. Grant is not poetic, but he asserts his early interest in horses and then, incidentally, reveals his growing competence in managing them at the same time that he shows their recalcitrant and potentially dangerous energy. Then there is trading in horses, in which Grant presents himself the dupe, since he tells the old trader at the outset how much his father has allowed him to pay for the horse in question. But if he is the fool of the trade, he nonetheless gets the horse he wants.

This is a fine bit of dry humor—very dry—and it is related to the kind of humor that Henry Adams observed in remembering Grant's witticism: "The best way to kill a bad law is to execute it." Adams knew that in Mark Twain's writing, the remark would have been hilarious; but in the voice of Grant the President, the remark was, if not devastating, at least disconcerting in the extreme. In the *Memoirs*, the humor is somehow winning in that it reveals Grant's awareness of his victimization (he goes on to observe how his folly made him the laughingstock in the town), and yet there is the confidence of the generating memoirist who has survived the ridicule to become famous. Grant can thoroughly afford to expose his youthful naiveté. Though he never asserts his mature confidence, it is implicit in his account; at the same time, and again implicitly, Grant reveals both affection and a trace of empathy for the shame-faced young trader. He can still feel the old wound in the humorous effect of revealing it. His account of having been tricked and, subsequently, ridiculed is not unlike Franklin's anecdote of being laughed at by his future wife upon his entry into Philadelphia—except that Grant has no such direct and neat revenge as Franklin had in marrying Deborah Read. He has instead, lying ahead in his narrative, all the strategies of a commander to scout out and waylay his foe with feints, probes, flanking movements, and frontal assaults that merely mask the larger design of getting at the enemy's rear. Yet Grant never betrays consciousness of the connection between that early and these later deceptions; if he did, the whole narrative would be different.

Grant, in a similar incident, tells of having worn his West Point uniform proudly on returning to his home town, only to be jeered for being a "sojer." How much that simple episode is related to his having appeared at Appomattox seemingly out of uniform! Yet, here again, no consciousness of the connection is registered. Indeed, throughout the narrative, Grant shows himself as having appeared sufficiently nondescript as to be unrecognized for what he was. He can from time to time talk with a soldier, even a rebel soldier; he can pause to discuss the war with an ardent secessionist; he can at once devastate a loyal Confederate woman in Virginia, with the news that Sherman has taken Atlanta, and, almost in the same breath, offer her the courteous consideration of the power of his rank—and not (it is well to discriminate) the rank of his power. For Grant's power is obscurely separate from his rank or his uniform. He is not in uniform so much as he *is* uniform; he is not a general, he *is* general, in the deepest meaning of the word.

Those early humorous anecdotes of the horse and the uniform could provide a reader who watched horses and uniforms throughout the book with an elaborate tissue of connection. Thus there are the horses Grant bought and later lost in the Mexican War—and was again laughed at by his superiors for his failure to maintain possession of his worthless horseflesh. There is the horse he rode desperately through crossfire at street intersections in Monterey, to get more ammunition. And though there may not be the account of the drunken ride on Kangaroo, there are the two times he was injured in falls from horses. Finally, there is the incident at Shiloh, in which Grant tells of being surprised by the enemy while riding with Generals McPherson and Buell, and how all three generals fled—Buell losing his hat on the ride. In a sentence that could well stand for laconic humor that shadows the simplicity of his style, Grant remarks, "He did not stop to pick it up." In the headlong flight, Grant's scabbard was hit and broken, and

McPherson's horse was panting as if ready to drop. On examination it was found that a ball had struck him forward of the flank just back of the saddle, and had gone entirely through. In a few minutes the poor beast dropped dead; he had given no sign of the injury until we came to a stop.[12]

He completes the paragraph with the summary facts, followed by a feeling: "There were three of us: one had lost a horse, killed; one a hat, and one a sword-scabbard. All were thankful that it was no worse."[13]

This is an example of the conclusiveness of Grant's style: summary assertion of the facts accompanied by laconic observation about the feeling. That dead horse, in the middle of things, would have to stand for all the dead horses in the war, yet Grant neither insists upon the synecdoche nor elaborates elsewhere on the screams of wounded horses during battles, nor the stench of dead ones afterwards. Instead, there is only this kind of episode in the steady sequence of incidents and events.

In light of all the horses that appear in the narrative, there is something deeply touching about Grant's acknowledgment of the poor beast's having spent its dying life getting McPherson off the field, and particularly so when one considers that McPherson would be killed on horseback before Atlanta. Grant briefly acknowledges the event much later in the *Memoirs*:

It was during this battle that McPherson, while passing from one column to another, was instantly killed. In his death the army lost one of its ablest, purest, and best generals.[14]

Such a passage provides a fine bridge from the simplicity and humor of the book to its simplicity and restraint. Grant never goes extensively into the interior tensions of battle, nor does he make elaborate nods to the sentiments of praise, morality, or patriotism. Yet in that one word "purest," by which he characterizes McPherson, we see the compression of true generalization.

Only in sporadic and widely isolated sentences does Grant reveal anxiety. He experienced it in the Mexican War, when he led his first charge. Though filled with fear, he says he lacked the moral courage to retreat. He mentions this same response in describing his approach to the enemy in Missouri. Leading his small contingent and fearing to ascend a hill he believes to hide the enemy on its farther side, yet lacking the moral courage to retreat, he goes over the crest, to discover that the enemy has retreated. From that experience, he says, he emerged with the knowledge that the enemy is always as afraid of you as you are of him, a knowledge profound enough to become a truth that carried him through all his subsequent battles. Grant's conception that forward movement into battle results from the absence of the moral courage to retreat is, to say the least, arresting. Following Henry Adams, we could say that in Mark Twain—who shared and expressed the same vision in relation to writing—the paradox is critically fascinating. But in Grant, the general and writer whose whole life moved, and is moving, forward with the ordered purpose of destroying the enemy, the laconic observation that the determination to destroy the enemy arises from the lack or absence of the *moral* courage to retreat is a paradox sufficient—the longer we brood upon it—to appall. Grant, of course, does not brood upon it but simply goes forward in his narrative, as he had gone forward in war, toward the execution of his purpose. Here again he discloses this enormous fact of life without allowing the consciousness of the fact to condition the consciousness of his narrative or distract him from pushing on. A lesser writer would have converted such consciousness into emotional emphasis upon the anguish and horror of life at war.

But here again Grant, though he reveals such anguish, never allows the revelation to distract him from his narrative. After the battle of Belmont, his first major encounter with the enemy in the Civil War, he tells of throwing himself on a cot, only to leap up again (such a textual moment will have to stand for his failure to disclose his behavior at the end of the first day in the Wilderness). And he has this to say of the night after the first day at Shiloh:

> During the night rain fell in torrents and our troops were exposed to the storm without shelter. I made my headquarters under a tree a few hundred yards back from the river bank. My ankle was so much swollen from the fall of my horse the Friday night preceding, and the bruise was so painful, that I could get no rest. The drenching rain would have precluded the possibility of sleep without this additional cause. Some time after midnight, growing restive under the storm and the continuous pain, I moved back to the log house under the bank. This had been taken as a hospital, and all night wounded men were being brought in, their

wounds dressed, a leg or an arm amputated as the case might require, and everything being done to save life or alleviate suffering. The sight was more unendurable than encountering the enemy's fire, and I returned to my tree in the rain.[15]

Brief as it is, this passage is unusually long for its kind in the *Memoirs*. Grant customarily spends but a sentence (and even these sentences are rare) to indicate the immense strain of battle and responsibility he undoubtedly lived with constantly for four years. Thus he writes, in almost a phrase, of his immense relief in finally getting his troops on the east bank of the Mississippi below Vicksburg, after months of failure and frustration. And he remarks the enormous anxiety he felt, as late as Petersburg, about the possibility of Lee's escaping and eluding the iron grip Grant had put round him. Finally, he mentions his terrible headache on the morning of April 9, 1865, only to have it immediately cured upon receipt of Lee's letter agreeing to discuss terms of surrender.

Then there is Grant's description of meeting Lee in the McLean house later that same day:

> What General Lee's feelings were I do not know. As he was a man of much dignity, with an impassible face, it was impossible to say whether he felt inwardly glad that the end had finally come, or felt sad over the result, and was too manly to show it. Whatever his feelings, they were entirely concealed from my observation; but my own feelings, which had been quite jubilant on the receipt of his letter, were sad and depressed. I felt like anything rather than rejoicing at the downfall of a foe who had fought so long and valiantly, and had suffered

so much for a cause, though that cause was, I believe, one of the worst for which a people ever fought, and one for which there was the least excuse. I do not question, however, the sincerity of the great mass of those who were opposed to us.[16]

Both Grant's restraint and his truth are evident in every line. There is the truth of his not knowing what Lee felt and the restraint to refuse to imagine it; and there is the truth, or at least firm confidence, of his knowing what *he* felt and the restraint to refuse to embellish it. Even in his evaluation of Lee's lost cause, Grant carefully interpolates the fact that it is his *belief*, and not necessarily the ineffable moral truth.

If the laconic humor, simplicity, and restraint of Grant's style at once qualify and define the clarity of the *Memoirs*, they do not reveal Grant's heart. There is always a two-front war that he sees himself having fought, and that he fights again in the act of writing his book. From the moment he entered the Civil War, he sees himself faced not merely by the Confederates in his front but harassed by enemies from the rear, in the persons of rival generals. He presents himself, of course, as a modest, relatively unassuming, and certainly unpretentious man, somehow swept forward into fame by vast forces beyond his control. As a reader, I have no doubt that he was such a man. His steady, straightforward prose, with its essential clarity, its slight laconic edge, and its fine simplicity of plainness—so different from Lee's style, with its equal simplicity, but a simplicity of humility—serves to allay any doubt about Grant's sincerity or accuracy of self-portrayal.

Yet there is Grant's ambition, and anyone who thinks

it was not a vaulting ambition would be foolish indeed. After all, here is a man who has been commanding general of one of the largest armies in history, then President of the United States for two terms (who sought with all his might a third term, and almost succeeded), presenting himself as a modest person thrust forward into destiny and history. Early in the book he gives fine portraits of Zachary Taylor and Winfield Scott, portraits which clearly foreshadow the contrast between himself and Lee. Taylor is capable, casual, and politically unambitious, according to Grant—a man who sits his horse with both legs on the same side and who eschews pomp and military formality. Scott, on the other hand, is immaculately dressed, politically ambitious, and very conscious of his own worth. Both are, in Grant's eyes, fine generals. Yet it was the unassuming and politically unambitious Taylor who, like Grant later, became President; Scott didn't. Grant would like to think that Taylor's modest informality, representative of the life of democracy, was the transparency through which the common people could recognize his merits and lift him to the presidency. And Grant clearly, and in all probability sincerely, believed that his elevation to the presidency came not from personal ambition but from a similar recognition on the part of the people.

Yet Grant's whole narrative runs counter to such passivity. Once Grant enters the Civil War, he immediately finds his real enemy to be Henry Halleck. To be sure, there is evidence, both in the *Memoirs* and elsewhere, that Halleck pointedly depreciated Grant, particularly in the early part of the war. But in making the conflict emphatically present in his narrative, Grant conceals from the reader (and, I think, from himself) just what it was that Halleck feared, or possibly saw, in Grant. Let us allow him Halleck's ambition that led him to be General-in-Chief in Washington. The point is that Grant uses Halleck in his own narrative—Halleck being happily (happily at least for Grant) dead—to mask from himself his own ambition. Besides Halleck there was McClernand, whom Grant sees as a politician-general pursuing the possibility of the White House. Now, twenty and more years later, Grant the writer, who has occupied the White House for eight long years, devotes himself to steadily exposing McClernand's ambition and potential insubordination. Grant all but makes it brutally explicit that, in Sherman and McPherson, he found allies sufficient to enable him to thwart, and ultimately rout, McClernand (it is worth remembering that McClernand was a Democrat). Let me be clear. I am not doubting Grant's estimate of McClernand, but emphasizing how he uses his two-front war as a representation of the force that thrusts him forward to the very presidency he would have us believe they coveted. This immense contradiction is not some concealed motive in the book; it is always all but on the surface of the narrative. It shows how the effective soldier-politician in a democracy shields himself from his own ambition by finding and attacking that ambition in his rivals.

The events of the war, cast in the deliberate sequence with which Grant narrates them, are the external force that preoccupied him in his march to power and fully occupy him as a writer, displacing the political life that lies between him and the lived conflict in which and through which he emerged as a recognizable and relentless military and political force. In recounting that life, Grant was, at the threshold of death, once more in touch with that fugitive part of himself that was, though fighting to be known, still unknown. His determination was thus undetermined. He was back in the field of force where his own acts were, on a terrain of vast contingency, still completing him.

It is no surprise that contingency is everywhere in the narrative. Grant sees it dominating the accounts of other memoirists. Thus he excoriates William Preston Johnston's Confederate account of Shiloh, on the ground that it is one big *if*:

> *Ifs* defeated the Confederates at Shiloh. There is little doubt that we would have been disgracefully beaten *if* all the shells and bullets fired by us had passed harmlessly over the enemy and *if* all of theirs had taken effect. Commanding generals are liable to be killed during engagements; and the fact that when he was shot Johnston was leading a brigade to induce it to make a charge which had been repeatedly ordered, is evidence that there was neither the universal demoralization on our side nor the unbounded confidence on theirs which has been claimed.[17]

Yet by the end of Grant's account of the battle, he too has been lured into the realm of the hypothetical, contending that if Halleck had let him proceed after the victory at Shiloh, all would have been different.

His entire narrative is fairly studded with similar resort to *ifs*: if it hadn't rained, if Halleck hadn't dissolved his command, if the victory at Donelson had been quickly followed up, if Anderson had not made his all-night march into Spotsylvania (barely beating the Federals to the crossroads), if Butler and W. F. Smith had made a swifter march upon Petersburg, if the

Northern press had not devoted itself to praising Lee, if G. K. Warren could have been persuaded to move, if Sigel had shown more initiative in the Valley. These *ifs*, all through the narrative, are the hypothetical defenses Grant to the last throws up as he pushes his narrative forward, toward what is at once the end of the war and the end of his life. They are nothing less than the wilderness thicket with which Grant flanks his forward progress. They tell us not only about the life of a general but about life in general, reminding us of the fragile man Benjamin imagined after World War I and reminding us, as well, of Grant's fragility throughout his life.

There still remains the forward progress of the narrative, a progress that is the very soul of Grant the writer. As Grant moves toward his end, he increases the incidence of the battle orders and letters he wrote at the time. These orders, dispatches, and letters show how great a writer he was long before he wrote his memoirs. At their best, battle orders are not merely the prediction of the future but the making of it. That is why Grant is careful to quote his own orders. Here again, he is in the utter convention of the memoir, but Grant's battle orders, such as the one he wrote to Buckner at Donelson, defined not only the end of that brief campaign, and not only "Unconditional Surrender Grant," but the end of the war—though that end would be three desperate and frightful years later. To see how frightful things had become, one has but to read the order Grant sent to Halleck (which he duly includes in his narrative):

I am sending General Sheridan for temporary duty whilst the enemy is being expelled from the border. Unless General Hunter is in the field in person, I want

Sheridan put in command of all the troops in the field, with instructions to put himself south of the enemy and follow him to the death.[18]

And Grant includes the dispatch he received from Abraham Lincoln, referring directly to that battle order:

This, I think, is exactly right, as to how our forces should move. But please look over the despatches you may have received from here, even since you made that order, and discover, if you can, that there is any idea in the head of any one here of "putting our army *south* of the enemy," or of "following him to the *death*" in any direction. I repeat to you it will neither be done nor attempted unless you watch it every day, and hour, and force it.[19]

Here his order to Halleck comes back upon him, and him alone, to take full responsibility to see that Early is followed to the death. Here is the full implication of having determined upon unconditional surrender far back at Donelson. Moreover, it comes at a time when Grant can see the possibility of the total defeat and annihilation of his enemy. If Lincoln, fully committed to his support, urges him on to the annihilation, it is Grant who, having originated the strategy, will have to pursue it personally to realization. No wonder that, as Grant faced Appomattox and Lee's ravaged army, he dreaded the annihilation that he had commissioned himself, and had been commissioned, to inflict. No wonder he had that terrible headache on the morning of April 9, when he waited through Lee's refusal to submit at once; and no wonder his headache was annihilated upon receipt of Lee's letter of willingness to discuss terms for "the surrender of this army." Spared by Lee from the responsibility of taking the full consequences of the strategy he had laid down, no wonder that he could be magnanimous.

Yet he *was* magnanimous—as magnanimous as he had been courageous in bearing the responsibility of his commission. And he is courageous in his *Memoirs*—courageous in executing them. There is a passage near the end of the book that seems to me to define Grant the writer. Asked by Lee at Appomattox to write out the terms of surrender, Grant describes how he faced his task:

> When I put pen to paper I did not know the first word that I should make use of in writing the terms. I only knew what was in my mind, and I wished to express it clearly, so that there could be no mistaking it.[20]

Here is a writer who has a force—note that he does not call it an "idea"; it is merely a *what*, it is in his mind, and he knows it. The words follow or are consequent to that energy, and they will express it clearly if it is clear in the first place, and Grant is sure that it is. Thus writing not only has order, it *is* an order, in the dynamic meaning of that word. It may be secondary to the clear energy behind it, but it is primary and directive to all who read it. Grant's *Memoirs* have that clarity.

Notes

1. William Faulkner, *Intruder in the Dust* (New York: Random House, 1949), pp. 194–95.
2. Ulysses S. Grant, *Personal Memoirs of U. S. Grant*, 2

vols. (New York: Charles L. Webster & Company, 1885), II:226.

3. Shelby Foote, *The Civil War: A Narrative*, 3 vols. (New York: Random House, vol.1, 1958; vol. 2, 1966; vol. 3, 1974), II:119.

4. Grant, *Personal Memoirs*, I:39.

5. Shelby Foote's account (*The Civil War*, III:184–86) is the most detailed and vivid.

6. Grant, *Personal Memoirs*, II:210.

7. Walter Benjamin, *Illuminations* (New York: Harcourt, Brace & World, 1968), p. 84.

8. Ibid., p. 94.

9. William McFeely, *Grant: A Biography* (New York and London: W. W. Norton, 1981), pp. 493–99.

10. Henry Nash Smith and William Gibson, eds., *Mark Twain–Howells Letters*, 2 vols. (Cambridge, Mass.: Harvard University Press, 1960), I:278–81.

11. McFeely, *Grant*, p. 501.

12. Grant, *Personal Memoirs*, I:353–54.

13. Ibid., I:354.

14. Ibid., II:169.

15. Ibid., I:349.

16. Ibid., II:489–90.

17. Ibid., I:363.

18. Ibid., II:317–18.

19. Ibid., II:318.

20. Ibid., II:492.

History and Its Enemies: Writers and the Civil War

WILLIAM S. McFEELY

for Joseph Harrison

History has its enemies. It is attacked on two fronts, and there is even danger from within. The first assault comes from the social scientists, who, with gray stealth and vast cunning, mock it as frivolous gossip. The wounds of this thrust are painful to the historian's scholarly pride, and once his work is brought to its knees there is no mercy. The assailant takes up his victim's task and the resulting work is unrecognizable as history.

Meanwhile, on the other flank, the novelists attack. On gold- and red-blanketed chargers, they seize the day and carry off the past for their own lusty purposes. This ravaging is more fun, but it too leaves scars. When the two marauders depart, the sliver of territory left to the historians is barren.

But we bruised historians are not without our strategies and I would like to expose the dim outlines of a modest plan of counterattack that is gaining adherents and may allow history to regain its ancient and honorable place in our literature. History was once the stories shared by a vast population, but recently its scope has narrowed so that too much of what is written as history is the work of experts talking to other experts. I do not want to overstate my case; there is, of course, history written by the most sophisticated historians that reaches a very wide audience indeed—Fernand Braudel's work comes to mind. In a different range, more immediately relevant to this essay, one thinks of the expert and accessible work of such fine historians of the American Civil War as Thomas L. Connelly and Emory M. Thomas. Unfortunately, not all the work that gains popular attention is of this quality; much of what does is picture-book patriotism of the worst kind. Such writing, of which the Civil War has been the subject of more than its share, has given narrative history a bad name and drawn off many serious historians into analytical work that is not popularly comprehensible.

In the nineteenth century, Francis Parkman, in splendid narrative style, could hold a large audience with book after book of history of the eighteenth century in which the struggle for a continent was played out. The contestants were not only the British and the French but also, vividly and importantly, the Iroquois and the Ottawa. Parkman's analysis of what he called the savagery of the native Americans may seem appalling to us today, but there is no doubt that he was dealing with important questions about different and contending cultures. And he wrote so well that his readers stayed with him, as they did with another amateur historian, General Grant. As James Cox has written elsewhere in this volume, Ulysses Grant in his *Personal Memoirs* took us through the vast complexities of a great war with a splendid sense of the whole of the terrible business.

Probably 300,000 people read that book, or at least, its account of the battle in which a person in their family fought and, possibly, was wounded and killed.

In the main, historians are not talking to their fellow citizens as effectively at the close of the twentieth century. Their work seems to have lost value. I am the first to concede that our century seems to be proof that no one ever learns anything from history, and yet I suspect that some members of the population at large (publicly) and the professional historians (recently) think we should keep on trying to do so. Marching under a modest banner, I think there is just a chance that, however embattled, historians can again find a useful way to inhabit history.

There will be no Wagnerian transfiguration in this victory. As is usual in these matters, the regaining of ground will involve compromises with our enemies. But I am not a Southern historian for nothing. I know what a good thing can be made of defeat. For public consumption, you despair of the lost cause while quietly bringing home the bacon. In the case of the defeated historians, the morsel to be recaptured is the fun of writing stories about the past.

Of the enemies, the social scientists are not much of a problem. It is perfectly obvious that their thunder should be stolen. The analytical work of the psychologists, anthropologists, and political scientists is essential to the historian as he does his own work. This discovery is not a recent one; Plutarch was using psychology when he wrote about Alcibiades. All the historian needs to remember is that he is a craftsman who is required to deal with discrete and changing happenings. He must be wary of generalizations about the sameness of human behavior and he must be skeptical of all claims to immutability.

But more than critical alertness is needed to avoid a concession to the social scientists of a monopoly in the realm of accuracy and truth. Clio must also zealously guard her virtue—must defend the word. The social scientist and the historian may be cousins, but they do not necessarily speak the same language. Each can and must use the other's tools, but the historian must remember to speak in his own voice. He must speak not in a structured, analytical language, understandable only to those trained to hear it, but in a language that is spoken in diners. There is often a fair amount of din in diners, and the historian must not add to it with a lot of extraneous sounds of scientific methodology. To take a simple but telling example, the historian has no license to present naked tables of figures. It is his job to multiply and divide them for us in words that we can hear and understand. He must do his own analyzing and then, in his own voice, tell us what he has found. The story he tells will, no doubt, be complex, but it must make sense.

The novelist is a more subtle opponent than the social scientist, and it is the historian's relationship to the imagination of fiction that I now want to investigate. Novelists and historians speak the same language. This fact did not come about because historians were forced to speak the invader's tongue—quite the contrary. When writers began calling themselves novelists and telling a particular kind of story, they were adopting a language that historians had been using since

Thucydides. And, to get back to basics, both the novelists and the historians had been taught to talk, if not to sing, by the poets—the bards. The people who listen to the novelist and the historian should be able to understand the words written by both. And yet there is a difference between the two writers, the difference between imagination and memory.

A fine historian once tried to teach me the difference between imagination and memory. During a rich but doleful conversation about the state of the historical craft, he hauled down an ancient edition of Thomas Hobbes' *Leviathan* and read from "On Man." There Hobbes, asking how we know ourselves, suggests that it is one thing to remember, in a simple fashion. In that mental effort, the modern historian would follow facts established either from experience or from documentary sources and, when examining a war and telling of, let us say, a cavalry charge, remember, in clear detail, a horse or a man. It is another thing to compound those memories and produce a centaur. That creature would be the imaginative work of a novelist, whose fictional realm is not necessarily mythical; he may well give us a more mundane character than Hobbes' centaur. But the novelist *does* live in a world in which he must do more than verify the actuality of the horse and the man on a given battlefield. He must make something of them out of the whole cloth of his imagination.

In *Gone With the Wind*, when Margaret Mitchell decided Scarlett and Rhett needed a final face-off, she placed them just where she wanted them: "The front door was slightly ajar and she trotted, breathless, into the hall and paused for a moment under the rainbow prisms of the chandelier." Mitchell imagined how Rhett would reply to one more preposterous proposal of Scarlett's—that this time she really did love him. When the heroine realizes that he isn't buying, and asks what she is to do with herself, he answers, "My dear, I don't give a damn."[1] (As a historian with a notoriously bad memory, I didn't trust myself to remember even that famous line correctly. I had thought he said, "Frankly, my dear, I don't give a damn"; perhaps Clark Gable did so in the movie. So, dutifully, off I went to the library to do my research and verify the quotation. If nothing else, we historians have our pedantry to distinguish us from the novelists.)

Had I, a historian, been faced with having to re-create—not imagine—the scene, I would have needed to check the hotel register in Savannah, or the account books of Rhett's business firm in Atlanta—or who knows what else?—to confirm that he was, indeed, at home that day. And I would have had to overcome all problems of literacy and discover the diary of Mammy, or Prissy, or Pork that said, "Mr. Rhett finally told her off this morning and used a good strong word in doing it." And even then, I would have had no license to use quotation marks for Rhett's remark. The best I could have done was say that, in no uncertain terms, Butler told Butler that he did not care what she was going to do in the future.

The historian faces dilemmas that are as silly as this. Getting a conversation right may be as important to him as it was to Margaret Mitchell. When I was working on my biography of Ulysses Grant, I had a conversation that I had to make work. Grant was already the victor of Vicksburg and Chattanooga when he was ordered to Washington to be put in command of all the Union armies, but he had not yet met his commander-in-chief, President Lincoln. I knew, from a photocopy of the hotel register, that Grant and his son had checked into the Willard; from a diary, that people had gotten up from their chairs and applauded when he came into the hotel dining room; from the newspapers, that he had walked around the corner and up the block to the White House. Grant was a bit on the late side for one of Abraham and Mary Lincoln's regular evening receptions. The next morning's papers were full of talk of the excitement that Grant's arrival had made, but they did not tell me what I wanted to know. How did the two men size each other up? What did they say to each other?

My curiosity was not just a matter of social chitchat. To a certain extent, it could be said that the future of the Civil War depended on how the president and the general worked together. All I had to go on for an account of their encounter was the diary of a cabinet member who disliked Grant on sight, and the oft told tale that Lincoln, hearing the fuss made by the crowd near the door, went over to the man who had just made his perfectly timed entry, and said, unastonishingly, "Why, here is General Grant."[2] I still do not know whether that was, in fact, what Lincoln said (or what Grant replied). But by then my research, coupled with my imagination, had taught me what Grant looked like and how Lincoln would have seemed to him—how Lincoln, from his great height, would have looked down on the small, gentle-looking man whom he had chosen to lead one of the most ferocious and bloody campaigns in military history. I could not make up any dialogue but I could say, with some confidence, that their brief conversation went just fine.

I had been working in Hobbes' world of memory and

imagination. Ancient as I am, I cannot recall from experience anything about my subject. I have never been able to work in contemporary history; for me, history is before the time that I can remember—before that evening when my father got off the commuter train and told my mother that Will Rogers and Wiley Post had been killed in a plane crash. What I was working with was historical memory, the documents of the past: formal letters between a president and a general and whatever informal material I could find. I was also, in the instance of the Lincoln-Grant meeting, relying more than I would have expected on the recollection of one old man, Jacob Gunn, a retired lead miner, over a hundred years old when I talked to him. He remembered, as a small boy, starting across a narrow footbridge in Galena, Illinois, looking up, and seeing the great General Grant coming toward him. Other than turning tail and fleeing, there was no escape, so he kept on walking, and as they came alongside one another, the boy did not find Grant at all frightening. "He was a little man, about my size," he said. Jacob Gunn was about five foot six or seven inches—and suddenly I knew something important about Grant that I had not known before. The factual matter of his height had taken on meaning. Certainly, or so it seemed to me, Grant's height and calm physical presence mattered when he first encountered the six-foot-four Lincoln.

I was using the memory of the historian. I could not make anything up, as the novelist can. I could not make Grant six foot nine anymore than I could make up sentences that I would have liked to have him say. I was dealing with *res gestae*, with things that were done, with something that *did* happen. Lincoln *did* meet

Grant and *did* so on March 8, 1864. I am uneasy when E. L. Doctorow, in his novel *Ragtime*, has Emma Goldman and Evelyn Nesbit Thaw meet, without evidence of their acquaintance. I am even more troubled that, when asked if the two women had ever met, he replied that they have now.

Am I being too severe? I guessed how my two men felt about each other quite as much as Doctorow did about his two women. Perhaps Doctorow can raise important issues—certainly he can raise amusing ones—even as he violates the past with his skillful game of imagined meetings of historical and fictional people. Can I, after all, make much of a claim to be discussing matters of true moment with my tale of what two celebrities, being fussed over in the White House, looked like or sounded like? Wasn't what was happening to the men on the battlefields far more important? Doesn't the novelist have a far better chance of imagining the pain of war—of understanding the history of emotion—than the historian, with his limited documents of memory?

To test this idea, I would like to take a brief look at three works of Civil War fiction, and a fourth work which is without a defined genre, and test a challenge that has come to historians, not from external enemies but from one of the best men in our ranks. In the preface to his brilliant book, *Southern Honor*, Bertram Wyatt-Brown wrote: "Through metaphor and felicity of language, the novelist's imagination can recreate the way people once thought and acted, so ordering matters toward an ethical veracity that the historian could never achieve."[3] It is my view that if we historians are thus excluded from any chance of reaching the only veracity worth its salt, we will indeed have demonstrated that we are defeated.

Some writers of fictional accounts of the Civil War have done their work exceedingly well. Ambrose Bierce, in "Killed at Resaca," has as his narrator an engineer on a general's staff who tells the story of the hero, Herman Brayle, an officer who is sent along the front line with battle orders. Lieutenant Brayle, we are told, "was more than six feet in height and of splendid proportions, with the light hair and gray-blue eyes which," Bierce adds sardonically, "men so gifted usually find associated with a high order of courage." A soldier, not so gifted, takes a hard line as Brayle sets out nobly across a battlefield with orders: "I'll b-b-bet you t-two d-d-dollars they d-drop him b-b-before he g-gets to that d-d-ditch!"[4] But Brayle makes it back safely.

The next time he is sent out, he moves on horseback across a field in clear view of the enemy riflemen. "He was a picture to see! His hat had been blown or shot from his head, and his long, blonde hair rose and fell with the motion of his horse. . . . An occasional glimpse of his handsome profile . . . proved that the interest which he took in what was going on was natural and without affectation."[5]

Was the fiction writer carried away with his gorgeous and observant hero? Are we doubtful about this picture of a Civil War battle? Yes, but not for long. We soon learn that this splendid damned fool provokes a needless exchange of lethal firing. The enemy riflemen fire at Brayle, their fire is returned, and the enemy artillerymen take it up and fill the air "with storms of screaming grape." Soon, on Brayle's side of the line, the trees are "splintered" and "spattered . . . with blood."[6] Men who needn't die, die.

The engineer-narrator watches the hero, now on foot beside his dead horse, looking calmly toward the enemy. He realizes that Brayle has come on a steep, narrow ravine that his horse could not have crossed. But it was so steep that had Brayle, on foot, jumped into it, he would have been safe. Suddenly, there is a cessation in the sharp firing, for Brayle has been killed. In a commemorative moment, men from both sides move out of their lines to bear Brayle's body back. Drums roll.

The narrator keeps Brayle's wallet, and some years later, in San Francisco, attempts to return a love letter that he found in it. He discovers Marian Mendenhall in "a handsome dwelling on Rincon Hill." She is "beautiful, well bred—in a word, charming." She takes hold of the letter: " 'This stain,' she says, 'is it—surely it is not—?' " Brayle's friend replies: "Madam . . . pardon me, but this is the blood of the truest and bravest heart that ever beat." But Miss Mendenhall is not impressed; she throws the letter in the fire and asks, "How did he die?"[7]

The friend (and narrator) has read her letter, written two years before the battle of Resaca, in which she had said:

> Mr. Winters, whom I shall always hate for it, has been telling that at some battle in Virginia, where he got his hurt, you were seen crouching behind a tree. . . . I could bear to hear of my soldier lover's death, but not of his cowardice.[8]

Suddenly, all of Bierce's claptrap about a heroism more noble than could possibly be human evaporates and the raw business of men and women, and fear and bravado that is the business of war are exposed. To impress a woman, safe on a hilltop in San Francisco, a man had caused other men to die and had been unwilling to take shelter in a ravine to save himself.

"I had never seen anything so beautiful as this detestable creature," declares the narrator; and in answer to her question, "How did he die?" replies, "He was bitten by a snake."[9]

The Red Badge of Courage, Stephen Crane's far more famous story about the Civil War, is also a study of cowardice and courage. (Henry Fleming, you will recall, has the sense, in effect, to climb down into a ravine and play with a squirrel—at least for a time.) There is splendid writing in the novel, including a description (which I envy) of an unnamed, watching general,

> seated upon a horse that pricked its ears in an interested way at the battle. There was a great gleaming of yellow and patent leather about the saddle and bridle. The quiet man astride looked mouse-coloured upon such a splendid charger.
>
> A jingling staff was galloping hither and thither. Sometimes the general was surrounded by horsemen, and at other times he was quite alone. He looked to be much harassed. He had the appearance of a business man whose market is swinging up and down.

Henry Fleming sneaks up to take a close look, and knows, without saying it, that the general, as Crane put it, is "unable to comprehend chaos."[10]

As arrested as I am by Crane's picture of the general, I suggest that we be skeptical of Crane's imagination, because in one important way his "memory" may be flawed. He was born after the Civil War was over and could not remember it experientially, as could Bierce, who fought with an Indiana regiment. Crane strives for authenticity imaginatively, but though his soldiers talk in a more natural, more realistic voice than the high-toned rhetoric with which Bierce's narrator speaks, Crane may not be getting us as near the speech of the Civil War soldier as he thinks. He is a fine novelist, but he is not as fine a historian. Diaries and letters tell us what we already know: Civil War enlisted men called their officers "shit-assed damned fools"; but in those same diaries and letters, men wrote in an elevated way of the "cause"—almost always undefined—in rhetoric very like Bierce's. There is also evidence in these personal writings of astonishing frankness in expressing the affection men felt for other men.

Crane, in 1895, did not dare let himself expose any such thing. (Or his editor did not; we now know that Crane's manuscript was much changed.) Crane was one of the most successful practitioners—Theodore Roosevelt was another—of the all-too-successful effort of Americans, at roughly the time of the Spanish-American War, to redefine masculinity. It was all cold baths and fear of homsexuality; it was a kind of "muscular Christianity" that has left us a nation of tongue-tied men in terms of expressing affection—or fear. The need to pose as always strong and confident prevents us from responding adequately to death and keeps us from telling the truth about an imperfect world. In the old edition of *The Red Badge of Courage*—the one that has influenced our view of the Civil War so strongly—Henry Fleming, when he overcomes his cowardice and carries the banner through the thick of battle into victory, is allowed a *gloria* very different from Herman Brayle's. There is no death at the edge of the ravine for him; he survives, is washed clean by the rain: "Over the river a golden ray of sun came through."[11] He is redeemed; American manhood is redeemed. He is not bitten by a snake.

Stephen Becker's hero is. His novel, *When the War Is Over*, is, like Bierce's, a story of needless death. After the Civil War ends, a barefoot country boy, who has fired on Union soldiers with his father's hunting gun, is condemned as a guerrilla and is ordered shot by one of the worst of what Stephen Crane called "jangling" officers.[12] To the historian who wonders what happened to the terrain he used to occupy, one of the most disconcerting aspects of this fine novel, by a present-day writer, is that the general is a real one, General Joseph Hooker. The incident is also real; there was a Billy Budd of a boy who was court-martialed and shot in the circumstances that Becker follows. The place is Cincinnati; the time is just after Appomattox. In Bierce's "Killed at Resaca," only the battle's name and the date of the letter place the events; in Crane's *The Red Badge of Courage*, even the hero scarcely has a name, and the battle and its date are not given.

Becker's historical memory gives us real names and events, but he does not merely do archival research into the case in order to give its precise details, nor does he build a social history of the boy's family or town. Instead, using a signal from history, he creates a history with his imagination. At the story's close, with no pardon from either President Lincoln or President Johnson, General Hooker—real—tells the judge: "Why, sir, when I was in command of the Army of the Potomac, Lincoln would not let me kill a man. Lee killed men every day, and Lee's army was under discipline; and now, sir, Lincoln is dead, and I will kill this man. Yes, sir, I will. The order is given to shoot him tomorrow, and he will be shot, and don't you interfere."[13]

The next morning, Thomas Martin—real—stands in the rain, in front of his coffin, his blonde hair plastered to his head, ready to die. One young officer, Ned Silliman—fictional—has been vomiting at the prospect of having to shoot the boy. He wants to refuse to obey the order; instead, he accepts an order to let someone else, Marius Catto—fictional—do the job in his place. Martin is shot. Halfway back to town, Silliman says, "Oh my God, Marius, I am nothing." "We are none of us much," said Catto.[14]

Mary Boykin Chesnut, a woman and a civilian, was, like Bierce, another participant in the Civil War who wrote beautifully about it. For a long time we thought that her vividly sharp images of individuals—her husband's valet, Laurence; General Hood; Jefferson Davis—were the result of a diary kept day by day through the war. She could have had no way of knowing how her story would come out, because the next day had not arrived. Her picture, surely, was more authentic than any imagined by a novelist. There was in her world, or so it appeared, no memory and no imagination. There was nothing but immediate impression. All of her characters are ferociously real—Hamptons and Elliotts and Rhetts. If you don't know their pedigrees, you have no business looking over her shoulder at her diary or imagining yourself at her dinner table. She told it exactly as it was. Or so early editions had led us to believe, before C. Vann Woodward demonstrated that she wrote the book twenty years after the war. She had an intermittent diary to use as notes, but, like Ulysses Grant, she depended most on her prodigious memory.

But she depended, too, on her imagination. She had tried to write novels, but they proved vapid. In her political mind, people had to be real. They had to have names people knew. So she could not, in the nineteenth century, be a novelist, and though well read, she had no scholarly bent, and being a historian probably never occurred to her. So she created her own genre, the imagined diary. The result is one of the most vivid and, I submit, truest pictures of the Civil War that we have.

If Bierce, Crane, Becker, and Chesnut put us in touch with veracity, do they exclude the historian from contact with it? Is there any important place left on the battlefield for the professional historian? Shackled to verifiable sources, can we do anything much except confirm that, for example, aides-de-camp *did* carry orders at Resaca? Does anything remain for us, other than checking up on the imaginations of other writers with our highly calibrated memories?

My answer, of course, is yes. I do not think we should leave the history of human emotion exclusively to writers of fiction, and just as emphatically, I do not think we should "use" bits and pieces of fiction to decorate our supposedly more solid work. We can write our own books; we too can re-create the past.

Sometimes our stories are long ones that can get us in trouble. Narrative history, with a larger span than a single battle or a single court-martial, is an object of scorn in some quarters, and with some reason. Too much of this work is pageantry rather than history. Nothing illustrates this better than the Civil War bookshelves crowded with what Edmund Wilson called "patriotic gore." We need no more of this, and its repudiation must be stern if history is to regain its self-respect. That done, narrative history should be kept, not discarded.

What is needed to scrub it up is a recognition that history is a democratic craft—in two senses. As the social historians have rightly insisted, it must be a history of people—of how people felt about what was happening to them—and not merely a study of the institutions that have so often frustrated and repressed them. It must be a history of privates and not just generals. (In my own defense at this point, I cite Mark Twain, who always knew that Ulysses Grant was, until he wrote his *Memoirs*, a confused soldier boy. The rest of the world mistakenly thought he was a certain kind of man, a general turned celebrity, a Julius Caesar.)

History must be democratic in another sense as well. To return to my earlier prescription, it must be spoken in the language men and women speak in diners. Semiliteracy and illiteracy present a huge challenge to our ability to be heard, but, like other writers, we should try to meet this challenge. In some basic, human way, people have an urge, in Robert Penn Warren's phrase, "to get their story straight." This is an ever-recurring need; the story is never gotten straight for good. But getting the story straight is exactly what history is all about.

Historians, skilled at particularities, should also give us a sense of the whole. An amateur historian, Ulysses Grant knew this, and so did Francis Parkman. We latter-day professionals need not be daunted by their ability to see a whole war, or decades of wars. Neither should we be patronizing about the unscientific quality of their work. They wrote about what mattered to them; they and we enter the past from the present. Their present was simply a different one from ours.

There might be better examples than the Civil War to suggest what new signals historians should be picking up, but let's see where in that well-worked world one historian's curiosity might take him. Reading Bierce's "Killed at Resaca," my fidgety mind might ask, Where and when was Resaca? It is a town in north Georgia, where Sherman fought Johnston; and Herman Brayle would have died on May 14, 1864. Bierce knew this, and although it did not matter to him, it does to me. I would go on and ask who else was at Resaca? O. O. Howard was there, and so was Wager Swayne; and my mind would have leaped (or stumbled) to another area of research. (With the luck of "good" amputations, they—unlike Brayle—survived to become, respectively, head of the Freedmen's Bureau in Washington, D.C., and in Alabama.)

Joseph Hooker was there too, and this fact would carry me to Chancellorsville, where he was in command and where—confused, scared, and perhaps drunk—he retreated after a terrible battle. It was this battle, unnamed in the story, in which Stephen Crane had Henry Fleming win his red badge of courage. And it was the fact that Hooker retreated back across the Rapidan that first made me worry about that splendid, but discarded, ending to Crane's story, a bit of which I recounted. Did the sun break through on *any* Union soldier after Lee and Jackson got through with him on that day? Here, my nasty historian's eye began to look askance at Crane's vision of the Civil War. If he (or his editor) had the end of the battle wrong, could he have nineteenth-century concepts of masculinity and courage wrong too?

Hooker's performance at Chancellorsville carried me, of course, to his fictional postwar behavior that doomed the pathetic hero of Stephen Becker's novel. I began to worry whether my negative judgments on Hooker were colored by Becker's treatment of him. Undoubtedly they were; one does not forget so vivid an image. But I disciplined myself and asked other questions about the general. How was it that Ulysses Grant, fighting in the wilderness only fifteen miles from where Hooker fought but a year later, reacted so differently to a similarly indecisive battle? At the day's end in 1863, Hooker, in his headquarters, was immensely agitated and ordered his battered and undisciplined Army of the Potomac to turn back, northward. In 1864, Grant, though troubled after an equally disastrous day, ordered his exhausted men to pick themselves up and drag themselves along, toward the south. My guess, when I was trying to analyze how men behave under the stress of battle, was that Hooker could see the Brayles, and the hundreds like him, fallen on the fields around him. Not all were dead; many screamed through the night in pain. Perhaps Hooker was too compassionate—or, more likely, too scared—to send them in for more. Grant, to my horror, could tune out such sights and sounds, could sleep, and the next morning could order his men forward.

Mary Chesnut also wrote hauntingly about Chancellorsville—and I could go on with examples of how, from a myriad of signals, the historian's curiosity can be aroused. He or she starts making connections, verifies the facts, builds the story. And in telling that story the historian cannot avoid the obligation to face the questions raised by what other people have told us about the past. Near the beginning of *Mary Chesnut's Civil War*, that splendid writer told a story of Laurence, her husband's manservant, and she placed him precisely: in Charleston, on April 13, 1861, during the bombardment of Fort Sumter. And she asked a question that, a century later, has kept a good many historians busy.

> Laurence sits at our door, as sleepy and as respectful and as profoundly indifferent. So are they all. They carry it too far. You could not tell that they hear even the awful row that is going on in the bay, though it is dinning in their ears night and day. And people talk before them as if they were chairs and tables. And they make no sign. Are they stolidly stupid or wiser than we are, silent and strong, biding their time?[15]

Willie Lee Rose is one historian who thought Laurence's sign could be read, if she did enough digging. In *Rehearsal for Reconstruction*, she looked at the sea islands, just outside that Charleston harbor. On November 7, 1861, the Union navy took Port Royal, causing the planters to flee and leave the slaves, who raised the islands' fine long-staple cotton, to fend for themselves. How they fended is what Professor Rose set out to discover. With diaries of teachers who went to the islands, and letters, but also with tax records and the products of a lot of other unglamorous archival searching, she came up with an answer to Mrs. Chesnut's question.

She did so by writing precisely the kind of history that, I argue, will recapture the field for us historians. And as Willie Rose wrote, she addressed what, finally, is an ethical question. Her good friend and mine, Bertram Wyatt-Brown, needlessly handed over his sword to the enemy with his concession that the novelist's imagination can re-create "an ethical veracity that the historian could never achieve."[16] As you see, I am not prepared to make any such surrender of *my* claim on that imagination, and as I read more of Thomas Hobbes I discovered that he, of all people, was an ally. As he made his examination of what he called the "wild ranging of the mind," the neat separation of memory and imagination began to yield. He became aware of "the dependance of one thought upon another."[17]

He then gave an example from his memory of English history. "In a Discourse of our present civill warre, what could seem more impertinent, than to ask [as someone with a historian's mind apparently did] what was the value of the Roman Penny?" But Hobbes was not troubled: "The Cohaerence to me was manifest enough." Signaled by the penny, he proceeded to liken the treason to his king to the "delivering up of Christ" for "30 pence." Strict historical memory—in this case the careful calculation by a forerunner of our economic historians—did not, alone, get him there. But that historian's particularity, coupled with something else— coupled with imagination—did. Hobbes, indeed, rendered a judgment: "*Imagination* and *Memory*, are but one thing, which for divers considerations hath divers names."[18]

As in the discourse on the English Civil War, there is attention to pennies in Professor Rose's study of *our*

Civil War. The particularities of history are there, for example, in her rigorous analysis of the economic dilemmas facing the freedmen; there is sharply acute psychological reasoning as well. In appropriately quiet voice, she splendidly met the definition that Thomas S. Hines recently gave to the history that I champion. He wrote: *"All* significant intellectual endeavor *has* to be analytical, though this need not be boringly advertised in every line. All good 'narrative history' must be analytical narrative, where the methodological paraphernalia pervades but never engulfs the 'story' and the 'drama.' "[19]

Near the end of her story—the war is over—Willie Rose has Laura Towne, one of the Northern schoolteachers who came to the islands to teach the freedmen, tell us about a meeting of the Republican party:

> At a meeting of Negroes, with only a handful of whites present, one man rose to say "he wanted no white man on the platform." He was talked down by one of his more generous fellows, who said . . . "What difference does skin make, my bredren. *I* would stand side by side with a *white* man if he acted right," and pleaded that the Negroes not be prejudiced "against their color." Another said, "If dere skin *is* white, dey may have principle."

There, Rose picks up the story:

> Laura Towne found it amusing. It was more significant than she imagined. The colored people were speaking the language of New England liberals, but the resentment of the member "who wanted no white man" was more widespread than the generous Miss Towne had reason to know. She had simply assumed that the whites would lead.[20]

Professor Rose extracted that scene from her historical memory, but she has employed her imagination with equal vigor. She knows what the room looked like, what the people looked like, and—a better feat still—how those people sounded. She hears all four voices: the three speakers at the meeting and Laura Towne, the reporter. And she has an answer to Mrs. Chesnut's question. Laurence, at least, knew what he was biding his time for.

In this small passage, I think we have a clue that may lead us to a reconstruction of history. If historians will cease to be intimidated by either the social scientist or the novelist, the field will be ours again. Then, with self-confidence, we can meet Hines' injunction that "history is both a science *and* an art."[21] If a coupling of science and art is regarded as unholy, too much should not be claimed for the bastard child. But the bar sinister can be an asset; humbly, the historian can avoid the worry of his novelist-parent over the definition of art. Instead, sticking to his craft and aware that he must tell his story in language his fellows of similarly lowly birth can understand, he has a fighting chance to achieve "ethical veracity." At the very least, he will have gotten his story straight. With his head held high at his writing table, he may even discover that those "enemies" with whom he has done battle were friends after all.

Notes

1. Margaret Mitchell, *Gone With the Wind* (New York: Macmillan, 1936), pp. 1024 and 1035.

2. William S. McFeely, *Grant: A Biography* (New York: Norton, 1981), p. 154.

3. Bertram Wyatt-Brown, *Southern Honor: Ethics and Behavior in the Old South* (New York: Oxford, 1982), p. xi.

4. Ambrose Bierce, "Killed at Resaca," in *The Collected Writings of Ambrose Bierce* (New York: Citadel, 1946), pp. 41 and 42.

5. Ibid., p. 43.

6. Ibid., p. 44.

7. Ibid., p. 45.

8. Ibid.

9. Ibid.

10. Stephen Crane, *The Red Badge of Courage,* in *The Work of Stephen Crane* (12 vols.; New York: Knopf, 1925), 1:77 and 78.

11. Ibid., p. 200.

12. Ibid., p. 38.

13. Stephen Becker, *When the War Is Over* (New York: Random House, 1969), p. 217.

14. Ibid., p. 231.

15. In C. Vann Woodward, *Mary Chesnut's Civil War* (New Haven: Yale, 1981), p. 48.

16. Wyatt-Brown, *Southern Honor*, p. xi.

17. Thomas Hobbes, "On Man," *Leviathan* (reprint of 1651 edition; Oxford: Clarendon, 1909), pt. 1, ch. 3., p. 19.

18. Ibid., pp. 19 and 20; ch. 2, p. 14.

19. Thomas S. Hines, letter to the editor, *New York Times Book Review*, October 3, 1982.

20. Willie Lee Rose, *Rehearsal for Reconstruction: The Port Royal Experiment* (Indianapolis: Bobbs-Merrill, 1964), p. 393.

21. Hines, letter to the editor.

The Great Tradition and Its Orphans, Or, Why the Defense of the Traditional Curriculum Requires the Restoration of Those It Excluded

ELIZABETH FOX-GENOVESE

Gnashing of teeth, beating of breasts, and righteous indignation variously distinguish discussions of our curriculum—or lack thereof. What has happened to our standards? What has happened to our culture? What are we teaching and why? Whom are we teaching and for what purpose? Can we justify spending the money of taxpayers and parents on the humanities, or on what was once known as a "liberal education"? Can we justify our claims as educators if we do not offer a liberal education? Perhaps above all, what has happened to the Great Tradition?

Even to talk these days of the Great Tradition invites confusion. For some of us, the phrase means little more than the history of Western civilization. For others it means more specifically the history of great ideas, or great books. For most, it probably means some combination of political and intellectual history—great men and great books. But it is probably safe to say that those who defend the importance of the Great Tradition to the curriculum view it as, in some way, central to our collective identity and collective sense of purpose. It is this commitment to the function of the history of Western civilization in our contemporary consciousness that makes its place in the curriculum so hotly contested. Unless I am very much mistaken, those who seek to restore the Great Tradition to its rightful place do not intend it to take its place as one "option" among many. They intend it to anchor the revitalization of our national cultural and intellectual and political life. And those who oppose its restoration in original form do not oppose a curriculum's including a history of Western civilization as one option among many; they oppose the claim that the Great Tradition constitutes the foundation of our identity, and they deny that it offers an adequate map for our collective future.

Anyone who has ever confronted a resentful beginning college student who, having been instructed to take one's survey course, responds "I hate history" has had to wonder why we teachers of history subject ourselves to this misery. The short answer is "to earn our salaries." The longer answer may vary from person to person, but is likely to include a love of history and a vague—probably ill-formulated—commitment to its importance. But whether we try to tell the resistant student that to know history is to love it, or that history is good for the character or the soul or the future paycheck, we have started the discussion on the defensive. Most of us, that is, tacitly accept the premise that education must justify its utility to the student, especially its economic utility but also, because the 1960s still cast a long shadow over our lives, its psychological relevance.

The recent bugle call of our new secretary of education, William Bennett, demonstrates that the arguments from utility and relevance will not go unchallenged. A growing number of educational leaders are publicly insisting that the "Great Tradition" can stand on its merits and, more to the point, can be forced down the throats of unwilling students as a condition of their access to the lucrative jobs they covet. The history survey can be restored to its proper place by fiat: It can be made a requirement.

I, being something of a cultural conservative and perhaps a bit authoritarian by temperament, am not opposed to requirements. I am especially not opposed to requiring one or more history surveys, for I both passionately love history and believe that it is good for the character, the soul, and our political life. But the arguments of those who would restore some putative "traditional survey" or "Great Tradition" make me uncomfortable. For they rest on the assumption that the SURVEY, in caps, has been graven in stone, sanctified by the generations, and, having been temporarily neglected, can be restored to its rightful place in pristine condition. Maybe it would be nice if it could, and I am no longer even sure of that; but it cannot.

By temperament an intellectual and cultural, though by no means political, conservative, I grew up on the comforting narrative of the Great Tradition as it was until very recently conceived. There is a pleasure in knowing the succession of kings, the rise of the bourgeoisie and the liberal tradition, the growth and triumph of humanism. There is another and related pleasure in knowing—preferably by heart—the uncontested great texts of our tradition. And I find those pleasures have been shared by others in conditions you might find improbable. For the past few months, I have been immersed in the diaries of antebellum Southern women, many of whom spelled imperfectly and punctuated yet more imperfectly. Yet many of these women sprinkled their private writings with unacknowledged quotations from Shakespeare: "slings and arrows," for example, abounds. And antebellum Southern men who went to college appear to have received a version of the history of Western civilization—notably, as formulated by Thomas Roderick Dew, president of William and Mary— that did not differ radically from what I was taught in the late 1950s and early 1960s—certainly differed little at all from what was taught at Harvard or the University of Wisconsin or the University of Virginia, or, for that matter, Smith or Vassar or Tuskegee in the 1890s or the 1930s.

That tradition, as embodied in the history surveys, began to collapse during the 1950s in the face of the insurgent instrumentalism displayed by American educators who rushed, after World War II, to get their share of the goodies that accompanied America's sudden position as the world's great and, for a while, only, superpower. Matters worsened in the late 1950s, when the Soviets beat us into space and set off a panicky race to turn every red-blooded American boy into a nuclear scientist, or at least an engineer. The *denouement* came with excruciating irony during the 1960s, when a politically naive, culturally radical generation declared war on the "academic establishment" by demanding "relevance"—that is, another form of the same instrumentalism. The student and faculty rebels, in effect, did the establishment's work for it: They completed the burial of the Great Tradition, along with the humanities in general. The quest for relevance and the revolt against authority in all forms, however, contained a more positive note: a broadening of the constituency for higher education—the unprecedented, if still inadequate, admission of women, blacks, Hispanic Americans, and others into the hallowed halls and sacred discourses of the academy. But the visible "radicalism" of the 1960s still shrouds their "invisible" contribution to the conservatism of the 1980s. The radicalism of the sixties, however shocking and painful to some at the time, lubricated the potentially painful changes in our society and culture—the advent of the age of the video, the Walkman, and the computer—that had been brewing since the Second World War. The common denominator—at the risk of oversimplication—must be sought in the personalism of both. But before I pursue that far-from-simple topic—too frequently cast as an accusation—permit me to reconsider the survey we have lost.

Unless I seriously misjudge, the sanctity of the survey, or the Great Tradition that it transmitted, derived from the assumption that it embodied the collective identity of civilized men and the collective values of civilized people. It assumed that members of the true polity and the republic of letters, who were overwhelmingly elite, white men, would acquire from the survey a sense of their proper identity and aspirations. They would learn not so much of cabbages as of kings, of the qualities of leadership and the perils of fortune, of statesmanship and character, of power and its corruptions, of civic duty and moral responsibility. The Great Tradition was fashioned by and for those who were to inherit the earth—not the meek, but the mighty. At its best, the Great Tradition introduced its heirs to a powerful set of values and to the perils of falling from those values. It offered a model of excellence and insisted that excellence comes at a price—and that, in the words of the record about Prince Valiant I listened to as a child, "freedom also has its responsibilities." The actors in the Great Tradition were a restricted group: Othello and Shylock paid the tragic prices of their race and their religion, respectively; Portia, who pleaded in fidelity to her modest woman's mission, but triumphed because of her outsider's ability to push the letter of the law to its logical extreme; but in her triumph reaped her reward by reassuming her subservient woman's role. Those excluded from the cast were invited to identify with its values, each according to its kind. That identification rested largely on submission to the proper order, to the dominance of others in matters political and moral.

I do not wish to take cheap shots, although the political and critical movements of the last couple of decades have generated the motives and skills for doing so. The Great Tradition sits like a duck on a pond, to be peppered by the buckshot of deconstruction and its votaries. Our skills have become those of cynicism, and we are rapidly losing the will or the ability to remember. But those who are asking us to celebrate and to honor mock us by their inability to remember and their refusal to understand anything. The Great Tradition cannot be restored as a blueprint for life in the fast lane. In all fairness, I do not think that Mr. Bennett intends it to be, but I fear that many of those who are rushing to support his initiative will. In the late twentieth century, it cannot be restored as a simple narrative of the triumph of truth and justice. It has more to offer as a record of the triumph of some people over others, of the cultivation of collective values at the price of many individual lives, and of the ways in which those privileged enough to do so wrestled with their angels, their demons, their honor and power in this world, and their salvation in the next.

The point is twofold: First, the Great Tradition that we have inherited was itself the product of a history; was made, not born—much less divinely ordained; and is, accordingly, open to visions and revisions. Second, that tradition was constructed by particular groups to serve their particular needs. It embodies one of the many possible narratives of our collective past—not all of them, not the only possible one. We have two elements to consider: the moment of vision and the viewers; the historical context in which the story was written and the tellers of the story.

Here, recent developments in philosophy and literary criticism have something to offer. And I must, in advance, beg the indulgence of the philosophers and critics for I am about to bowdlerize, or at least vulgarize, their sophisticated work beyond their recognition. In my own defense against their probable reactions, however, I must insist that their work in its original sophistication frequently defies the recognition of others.

More's the pity, for they have something important to teach. Crudely put, they insist, in this echoing common sense, that no story (they would prefer "narrative," but "story" will do) is either innocent or transcendent. No story, that is, can be told without some intervention on the part of its teller, without the teller's intentions shaping the choice of characters, the sequence of events, or the ending—or, what amounts to the same thing, without a heavy dose of implicit or explicit interpretation. No more than the camera faithfully and directly records reality do storytellers "tell it like it really was." And no story—we can, for purposes of this discussion, grant exception to the fundamental religious texts—tells it like it always will be, presents human affairs from the perspective of eternity. Stories belong to the living, to communities, to nations—yes, to civilizations, with all their tensions, imperfections, needs, and aspirations. They constitute compromises between things as they are and things as they ideally should be. Master—and, we might add, "mistress"—stories figure among the most important aspects of any individual's or group's consciousness. They order past experience to permit future action. They are indispensable. And the privilege of telling "official" stories ranks among the most important prerogatives that a community can afford any of its members.

The Great Tradition figured as one of, if not *the*, premier story of our civilization from roughly the end of the eighteenth century until the Second World War. And even when presented in the form of "Western Civilization" it carries a special importance for citizens of the United States, for it has provided the contours of a key official story throughout most of the life of our republic. We, collectively, embody its most privileged aspirations. We, collectively, represent the first great triumph of "progress," "individualism," and "democracy" over feudalism, barbarism, bigotry, and all the other forces of darkness against which the Great Tradition was forged. But its special resonance for us makes us specially vulnerable both to its prestige and to its distortions as collective autobiography. It is as if the developments of the 1960s had taught us that its claims to the status of official autobiography constituted a tissue of lies, consisted in the claims of the few rather than of the many. We, the people of democracy!

We feel betrayed. We do not, of course, put it that way. But we seem prepared to toss off any attempts to teach the Great Tradition as the remaining shred of that European authoritarianism and artifice that we began our national career by rebelling against. (I do not, by the way, mean to suggest that the Western European countries are not experiencing their own version of our present crisis, but it is their own, differs in significant ways from ours, and cannot concern us directly here.) Or, perhaps even worse, to reduce the survey to one option among many, to the kind of pre-tour lectures that alumni associations are wont to offer those whom they can persuade to travel in groups to Europe. Our attitude suggests that, for whatever reasons, we have dismissed what was once our official story as irrelevant, although whether irrelevant to most of us individually or irrelevant to the collective business of our republic remains unclear. And our attitude also suggests that we had been mesmerized by the story's claims to official status—that we too uncritically embraced it as either innocent or transcendent. As the product of a specific historical moment and a specific group, the story permits—some would say requires—revision. But its inadequacies for our present purposes do not cancel out our need for some story of our collective past.

I grew up on history. No surprise, if you consider that my father was a professional historian who was uncommonly interested in the mind and education of his oldest child, and who, long before "shared parenting" was named as such, took charge of me for the long hours between 4:00 and 8:00 in the morning. We were early risers; my mother was not. We began, when I was about two, with simple stories. As the years progressed, we went on to more complicated ones, introduced maps, charts, and classic texts. Before I had finished college, we had started to work on Arnold J. Toynbee's *Reconsiderations*. Heady stuff for a mere girl, but I loved it. It did not, in those days, occur to me that my identification with the people and events that were unfolding before my imagination was of primary concern. Although I *did* harbor a special fondness for Queen Elizabeth I and even a sneaking ambition to be the first woman President.

But I uncritically accepted the terms of the discourse as it was presented to me: The name of the game was power, the exciting story concerned who rules whom, how, and why. I was entranced by the Capetian kings, who managed simply to have surviving sons, to crown them in their lifetimes, and thus to secure the succession to the throne—in short, to build a state. I found the intrigues of the popes delightful. I marveled at the development of the canon law, which I certainly did not understand. I trembled vicariously at the wrath of the Hebrew prophets. I pondered the vicissitudes and fanaticisms of the religious wars. I cheered the victors of the French Revolution, never suspecting that in those days when the modern world was a-borning some women also tried to claim their rights. I never heard of Mary Wollstonecraft, which was a great loss. I shivered at the intrigues of Bismarck, torn between outrage at his insolence and admiration for his success. And more.

In retrospect, I can see that I was torn by contradictions that I had no words to express. When my younger brother and I began to share reading and to act out the stories we read, the only question in the assignment of roles was who would be the bigger boss: Who would play King Arthur and who Launcelot; who Athos, Porthos, Aramis, or d'Artagnan; who Robin Hood and who Little John?—although I did occasionally persuade him to play Maid Marion. Guinevere was not on my list, and I did not know enough about Morgana LaFey to understand what her special powers might be. A young friend of mine now writes her own stories, finding those available entirely unsatisfactory, and her hero, Princess Taraveev, leaves her husband the prince at home while she goes out to slay dragons, monsters, and wicked kings. But this is a new generation. I did not give much conscious thought to women's having been excluded from the roles that I admired, even less to what the implications of their exclusion might be for me. I suspended my disbelief and identified with the causes, the values, the characteristics of my heroes— claimed, in some measure, the tradition as my own. But then, I took great delight in simply knowing the story, in understanding how we had come to be what we were. The structure of the events and my ability to grasp it alike pleased me. I appropriated the tradition in some sense as my own, even if I could not face that my own kind, in the direct sense, had been largely excluded from it.

I also grew up on another kind of history, on what we might today call variously "oral" or "women's history." For that history, I am indebted to my grandmother, with whom I spent roughly a month of every year. Born in 1880, she was the repository not merely of the fascinating events of her own life, but of many previous generations of family lore. With her, I explored and settled in the Cumberland country and Shenandoah Valley, crossed the prairie, scaled the passes at Pike's Peak, witnessed the premature deaths of children in a large family, hemmed sheets by stretching them the length of a staircase, made bread, taught in a one-room schoolhouse, joined women's clubs, fought precociously for recreation facilities in a Middle America community, taught immigrant children to read, and more. Her history functioned in a direct sense as an extension of my autobiography. I felt myself especially heir to her struggles and her values.

It came as a great shock to me to learn, when somewhat older, that she voted Republican. I knew by then that some of her family had been staunch Free Soilers and abolitionists. I did not know that the party of Lincoln had become the party of Dwight D. Eisenhower, had opposed the party of Roosevelt and Truman. Still less did I suspect that an occasional social prejudice, such as anti-Catholicism, might accompany her upstanding and otherwise generous values. Nor did I know that on one occasion she had sorrowfully defied my grandfather—at the time chairman of the local Republican party—to vote for Franklin Roosevelt.

Today, many history teachers find that students who otherwise "hate history" respond enthusiastically to the opportunity to write a family history or an autobiography; find that students "come alive" when invited to construct an oral history. Suddenly, history acquires that personal dimension, comes home to them, takes on meaning. History in the personal mode becomes relevant. And it is true that I could not easily relate my grandmother to the Great Tradition, although, had I been more knowledgeable or wiser, I might have, since a particular strand of Protestant Christianity lay at the core of her identity. At her funeral, we read from Proverbs, chapter 31: "Who can find a virtuous woman? for her price is far above rubies . . . ," and sang the "Battle Hymn of the Republic." These choices correctly reflected her sense of herself, how she located herself in the world. The choices also reflected the public values encoded in the Great Tradition.

Two sets of stories thus presided over my initiation as a historian. In the beginning, I did not insist that they meet, but more or less easily tolerated their coexistence in my imagination and intellectual life. Of such coexistence, you may shrewdly observe, is schizophrenia made. And the recent disenchantment on the part of many with the Great Tradition derives in no small measure from their recognition of the schizophrenia. "Who needs it?" as they say. The recent developments in black, feminist, and ethnic scholarship have sharply—I should say irreversibly—challenged the Great Tradition's claims to be "everybody's autobiography." Clearly it is not. You can get to the middle of the nineteenth century (depending on the course), even until the final quarter of the twentieth, without being offered a woman, a black, or a Jew worthy of serious emulation or who speaks for the tradition as a whole. Oh, you can get your odd Joan of Arc, your Queen Elizabeth, your Hebrew prophet (providing that the course includes the Judeo part of the Judeo-Christian tradition). But how many surveys of the Great Tradition seriously propose such figures as embodiments of a distinct gender, or of minority groups? How many acknowledge that the tradition itself resulted from a clash of values and that the losers, or the excluded, might have had their own perspective on the story?

Frequently it is said—or perhaps worse *assumed*, not said—that the Great Tradition has been established on the basis of quality. Elite men just happened to produce the best and most serious work; elite men just happened to secure the leadership of states, movements, religions. There is no bias here, only recognition of quality—and the way things were. This position rests on a partial truth. Elite men did their best to monopolize the sword and the pen, and to secure that monopoly they threw in the right to tell the story as well. The right to tell the story proved decisive, for it permitted the victors of history to present their spoils as the desserts of individual skills and excellence. This is the quality part, and it emphasizes individual talent. The part about the way things were is more problematic. For in focusing on the individual, the tellers of the tale dropped the bit about the very few individuals who were permitted to enter the lists at all.

Let me be blunt. The Great Tradition, in its various guises, takes for granted that the pool of potential heroes was restricted to white, normally elite, males. If the tradition considers the reasons why some failed and others succeeded, it does so within the framework of individual ability and character, not within the framework of group membership. It includes the occasional improbable success story—the odd peasant lad who rises to the position of advising kings or popes, who produces a splendid text—but never so much as admits that some groups of individuals suffered systematic exclusion from exemplary roles. This, if I understand what is happening, is at the core of the many's rejection of the tradition as their own. On one level, the proponents of ethnic and women's studies have a point: in its official guise it is not their own.

Mr. Bennett proposes that we "reclaim the legacy," but does not explain how we persuade our people to recognize the legacy as their own. Professor (and Rabbi) Jacob Neusner, a conservative whom President Reagan appointed to the National Arts Council and who, as a Carter appointee, served on the National Endowment for the Humanities, recently wrote in William Buckley's *National Review* of the compelling claims of ethnic studies, notably black and Jewish, upon our national attention. Professor Neusner can hardly be charged with a radical quest for relevance, much less with a willingness to undermine high intellectual standards. A distinguished scholar, his commitment to intellectual rigor brooks no challenge. A convinced conservative, his commitment to society's collective moral and political responsibility defies question. I am loath to put words in Professor Neusner's mouth, but think I can fairly translate his remarks as a plea that we recognize that our legacy is plural, not singular, a plea that we accord proper weight to the contributions of various traditions to our collective tradition. But let me leave his forceful case in his own hands and suggest that you read it for yourselves. Instead, let me turn to the case of gender— the necessary place of women in any reconstruction of our collective legacy.

Women's studies, like various forms of ethnic studies, and indeed like the social history of the common people, have developed in large measure as a revolt against the claims of the Great Tradition to reflect the values and legacy of society as a whole. During the past decades, scholars, especially women scholars, have uncovered a vast amount of information on women. Although much remains to be done, we are beginning to have the rudiments of a history of women, and the hard truth is that history bears little immediate resemblance to the history that has been taught as the Great Tradition. The gap resembles the gap between the histories that I learned from my father and from my grandmother. In the first place, much of women's history *does* concern private, or at least mundane, matters: the bearing and raising of children, the cooking of food, the carrying of water, tilling of the soil—a great deal of hard work and the ubiquitous risk of death in childbearing. In other words, much of women's experience has not been of much concern to those who have written history. And if many women have demonstrated deep commitment to the religious values of their society—and to its churches, which is not precisely the same thing—those values and those churches offered negative, or at least passive and subservient, views of themselves as women and precious few opportunities for leadership.

In the second place, and more surprising, women's history has also addressed public as well as private affairs, and has revealed that women have engaged in the most dangerous employments, including military action. They have participated in, and even led, a variety of riots and protests; have exercised political power; and have attempted to participate in the most advanced culture of their societies. No woman has ever been pope, but short of that, women have done almost everything that men have done, albeit not as regularly. And "regularly" may be the key, for if individual women have proved their abilities to accomplish almost anything, women as a group have not been viewed as capable of such accomplishments. Worse, women as a group have been, to the extent possible, excluded from the opportunity to prove their excellence according to their society's most prestigious definitions of excellence.

The harsh lessons about women's place in society as women, about Western civilization's prevailing attitudes toward women, have convinced a significant group of feminist scholars that the Great Tradition has nothing to offer them. Mr. Bennett has asked us to reclaim our tradition's struggle for the ideal of justice, a plea to which some feminist scholars would doubtless respond that the project deserves their attention—but must inevitably result in women's rejection of previous ideals of justice. In this respect, the defenders of the Great Tradition are reaping the whirlwind their predecessors sowed. For if the Great Tradition has been less than hospitable to women, much of the scholarship on women that has developed in recent years has been resolutely hostile in return. In extreme form, the argument runs that the Great Tradition has always been militantly male and that it has silenced, even brutalized, women—"Women of Ideas and What Men Have Done to Them," to borrow the title of an encyclopedic history of women's intellectual work. But this extreme view does not merely dissect the "misogyny" of the tradition, it explicitly challenges the standards of quality on which it has been based. According to the logic, men began by controlling women's bodies and went on to control their minds, silence their voices, and trample upon their values. The very ideals of quality that the tradition embodies result from the struggle between men and women, or from men's determination to control women. The standards are neither innocent nor transcendent. They result from history itself: They are indeed the spoils of the victor.

This line of reasoning, which I in part follow and in part reject, leads, in its extreme form, to affirmation of an entirely distinct women's tradition. Women, so it is argued, speak "in a different voice." The generalizations concerning women's "difference" cloak a host of specific claims. Let me give you some examples. Women—this is the most common example—devote their lives to nurturing life and, accordingly, hate war. Either innately or socially given to so-called "maternal thinking," women are explicitly or implicitly pacifists. Women identify primarily with other women, rather than with men. Women are less likely than men to engage in the violation of nature: since the early glimmerings of industrialization in the sixteenth century, there has been a natural affinity between women and what we now call "ecology." Men, not women, have burrowed into the bowels of (Mother) earth, have turned waterways from their natural courses, have raped the land. Women write differently than men, not merely about different things, but in a different voice. Women have been less attuned than men to the modes of self-assertive individualism, in part because its privileges have been denied them. But leave the causes aside for the moment: Women have been less likely than men to say or write "I" with conviction, much less with anger. Women shroud their judgments in "silences." In political action, women are more likely than men to defend the needs and claims of communities, including small children, and less likely to embark on conquest either personal or collective.

This line of thought, at its most sophisticated, say in the mind of an Elizabeth Janeway, leads to a systematic critique of power as it has been used and abused by the great political figures of the Western tradition. It argues that women have specialized in the "powers of the weak." In sum, the attempts to identify a specific women's tradition have, by and large, resulted in the identification of women with the values of nurture, pacifism, collective life—the diametric opposites of what are taken to be the values of men, especially as encoded in the Great Tradition. Therefore, many women are tempted to retort to the plea that we reclaim that legacy with a defiant charge that since men have forged it, let them keep it if they choose. It has nothing to offer women. Indeed, it may have nothing to offer humanity, which it has brought to the brink of a nuclear holocaust.

There is an irony in this view of women's collective identity and collective dissent from the reigning truths encoded in the Great Tradition. For the women who oppose the tradition are, in large measure, espousing the view of themselves that it propounds. Shakespeare portrays Portia as triumphing, in the name of mercy, in a situation in which the unmediated claims of justice would have required delivering up the pound of flesh. Sophocles depicts Antigone as championing the principles of family religion—of clan and kin and their gods—against those of the state. And he carefully identifies the conflict of laws with a conflict between genders: if Antigone can thus "flout authority / Unpunished, I [Creon] am woman, she the man." And again: "No woman shall be master while I live." In the event, Creon's victory—the victory of the *male state* as the preserve of order—proves Pyrrhic indeed. Yet Sophocles casts the tale of Antigone's rebellion against that order as a tragedy, because of the legitimacy of both sets of claims. She lost because the claims she represented were archaic, impeded the progress of civilization. Creon also lost because he could not find a place for them in the new order he was trying to build.

But there is a second irony as well, for many of the women about whom we have the most information did not fit the mold at all. All that Queen Elizabeth I had in common with the myth of womanhood was her virginity—which itself was surely a myth. Catherine de Medici, Catherine the Great, Rosa Luxemburg, Dolores Ibarruri (the "Pasionaria" of the Spanish Civil War) were pacifists? Hardly. And they are only a few exemplars of a venerable tradition of battling women that includes poor women who have rioted for bread and against taxes since time immemorial. Social history abounds with women, not all of them patient Griseldas.

Here is the rub. The events that have produced the

feminist critique of our prevailing attitudes toward power have also produced a resurgent interest in social history: "history from the bottom up" or "the history of the common people" as it is variously known. To be sure, much of the new social history has been developed by men on the same male-centered principles that govern the Great Tradition, but social history has incontestably proved more hospitable to women than its high-culture, high-politics counterpart. And social history shares with women's history the temptation to dismiss the Great Tradition as irrelevant. Social history also suffers from the same problems of interpretation and of establishing significance as the Great Tradition. Suffice it to say that were one to substitute the new social history for the Great Tradition, one would be able to include considerable information on those whom the Great Tradition has excluded. But in my opinion, the substitution of social history for the Great Tradition would not solve the problems—would probably only defer them. We inevitably return to the problems of interpretation and point of view: to the problems of who is telling the story for what purpose. And unless we propose to give up on some meaningful political life entirely—unless, that is, we propose to leave our future in the hands of malevolent fates—we are condemned to take the function of the Great Tradition—of our collective intellectual and political legacy—seriously.

For the past few years I have been directing a large project "to restore women to history" by introducing materials on women into the basic American and European survey courses, and, by any normal standard, the project has been successful. It has also taught those who have worked on it a great deal about the difficulty of the problems and the choices. And, as in selecting illustrations for a story, the preeminent problem is choice. At the simplest level, the choices concern which parts of the "material" the instructor chooses to "cover." You can, for example, decide to include, or to exclude, information on women's participation in the English Civil War—just as you can include information on the members of the Model Army but exclude the Levellers, include information on the Levellers but exclude the Fifth Monarchy radicals, and so forth. The story of the French Revolution can and has been told with only passing reference, or none, to the women who played such an important role in its unfolding. You can also argue that a survey course—the Great Tradition—leaves little time for discussion of every little radical sect that happened along. What we want, after all, is a sense of the logic of events, of the outcome, of the abiding legacy. And I can counter that the stock figures of the story—the "great leaders," if you prefer— took account of those radical sects, and assuredly took account of the disorderly women who plagued their political lives, in making the decisions that we are told are worth remembering. To consider the decisions independently of the context in which they were made is to denigrate the great figures themselves, by ignoring the stern challenges they had to master. Worse, it is to obscure the important causes of actions in time and place. It is—and I trust you will pardon my incursion onto a sensitive contemporary terrain—to discuss the pros and cons of bombing abortion clinics without reference to religion, or politics, or capital punishment, or the lives of women. I am decidedly *not* taking a position on abortion, which I regard as one of the most agonizing issues in our society; I am merely pointing out that all positions on issues reflect the complexity of the societies in which the issues emerge.

The choice of whom to include in the story is difficult but soluble. Neither stalwarts of the Great Tradition nor extreme feminists may like the results, but it can be done. And it yields a refreshingly complex story. For women figure dramatically in the history of Western civilization, albeit not always in the ways any of us might have thought or wished.

In the French Revolution, women participated in, and frequently launched, some of the most portentous popular uprisings; women organized the *salons* in which many of the liberal ideas of the day were developed and disseminated; a woman, Charlotte Corday, killed the popular leader Marat; another woman, Mme. Roland, prodded, poked, loved, and otherwise shaped the members of the party of the Girondins; yet another, Marie Antoinette, embodied everything that different people most opposed or most wanted to defend; and yet another, Olympe de Gouges, drafted a statement on the rights of women that earned her the scaffold from those spearheads of revolution, the Jacobins. Different revolutionary groups held very different positions on the "woman question," the disposition of which played an important role in the ultimate outcome of the Revolution. Almost all the revolutionaries, with the possible exception of that quintessential *roué* Danton, had strong views about the proper place of women in society and the importance of that place to any society worth living in. Almost all of them also agreed on the necessity of women's subservience to men, but they disagreed mightily on the nature of the subservience and to which men it should be due. To teach the French Revolution as an exclusively male story is not merely unfair to women, it *distorts* the French Revolution. And the same obtains for almost every topic normally covered in any survey of the Great Tradition.

The exclusion of women from the Great Tradition has been a matter of choice. Their restoration to it is long overdue. The perplexing questions pertain not to exclusion or inclusion, but to the terms of inclusion. If we are to retain some semblance of the Great Tradition as our collective legacy, as the cornerstone of our identity—all the more if we are to insist that the tradition reflect what we consider the highpoints of that legacy, and that it must consist in something more than a random sample of autobiographies or family histories—then we must revise our story. I am by no means suggesting that we simply substitute social history for political and intellectual history, although I believe that politics and intellectual life can only be understood within their social context. I am suggesting that we restore gender to its rightful place as one of the basic categories through which we understand our experience and evaluate our past. I also fear that gender constitutes a good deal *more* than stalwarts of the tradition want to deal with and a good deal *less* than many feminists think is women's due.

By "gender," I mean, quite simply, what a society presents as the way to be a man and the way to be a woman—and the proper relation between the two. Gender is nothing more nor less than a social—or, if you prefer, cognitive or epistemological—category.

Gender tells us little, if anything, about individual perceptions or feelings. Gender belongs in the realm of language. It offers a structure for personal experience. The structure may be social, economic, political, intellectual, even, perhaps, psychological.

Gender organizes experience from the perspective first of society and second of the observer of society. To introduce gender as one of the essential ways of telling the story of the past will not distort the past. It will not substitute a problematic women's culture for what we have been taught to regard as high culture. It will not create more women generals and popes than we know there to have been. It also will not transform bellicose women princesses into closet pacifists and maternal thinkers. It will not, in short, radically transform the past we have inherited. But it will radically revise our view of that past—radically revise what we accept as innate or natural, how we assess different groups' opportunities to display excellence. Above all, it will revise our view of what was necessary and why. And our attitudes toward historical necessity determine our attitudes toward our own possibilities for creating a good society.

Make no mistake. To introduce gender into our reading of great texts and great political events is to increase, rather than decrease, our fidelity to the experience of our predecessors. Being closer than we are to societies in which gender constituted the fundamental principle of social organization, they were, if anything, more aware than we of the ways in which it impinged on any attempt to conceive the good society. With the passage of centuries, those who made the Great Tradition came more and more to define the polity and the republic of letters—those monuments of the good society—as male. They also tended to associate the forms of worship and organization that they were leaving behind—Antigone's clans and gods—with women. The tradition contains a good deal about the triumph of male rationality over female disorder. I warned you that we might not always *like* the story. My point is that we need to know it.

As a child, I now recognize, I was guilty of a horrible failure of imagination. I could not understand the fuss about adopted children's wanting to know who their real parents were. From my perspective, anyone who had parents, adopted or not, and a good home should be smart enough to let a good thing be. The existential question, "Who am I?" moved me not at all. It was difficult enough to work with the world you had been given—why bother about the worlds "we know not of"? You will recall, from the beginning of these remarks, that I also did not want to know that I could not realistically aspire to the roles, all male, with which I tended to identify. I think I have learned that I was wrong on both counts. And, further learned that both kinds of being wrong are related, and are related to the future of any justification for teaching the Great Tradition.

The Great Tradition earned its place in our education on two grounds: its creators and exponents presented it simultaneously as our collective history and as our autobiography. The political and social changes of the recent past have exposed its claims to be our autobiography as outrageous and fraudulent. And the erosion of those claims has reduced its claims as collective history to frivolity. Much of the revolt against the Great Tradition has been fueled by the refusal to accept someone else's autobiography as our own, and by the insistence that—whatever the world may say—our *own* autobiography matters. Both these responses command respect: The orphan—even the secure, adopted child—*does* need to know who he or she is. However painful the knowledge, orphans need to know—at least must try to know—who their parents were, and what their special legacy is. One can only admire the courage that can face those anxieties squarely, especially when the coveted knowledge is likely to demonstrate not that the real parents were dukes or counts, but that they were unfortunates who had a drinking problem, or not enough money to get married, or worse.

Similarly, those who have been excluded by the Great Tradition—and here I refer particularly to women, but they are not alone—need to know why. They need to know why they did not win, why they lacked the power or the resources to impose their views, why their kind did not tell the story. Here, as with real-life orphans, I am suspicious of the romantic answers. I doubt, for example, that all women shared a distinctive culture and opposed the reigning values of their societies in a consistent and programmatic fashion. But my real point lies elsewhere.

I am deeply committed to the recovery of women's past. I also believe that the recovery of that past will illuminate and transform our reading of the Great Tradition. It will not substitute for it. No one's autobiography can susbstitute for our collective history. Nor can any of us hope to reconstruct our autobiographies without such a history. We cannot reclaim the legacy of the Great Tradition unless we understand and revise the purposes for which it was constructed. It is neither innocent nor transcendent—above all, not graven in stone—but rather, as Rousseau said of the Constitution, engraved in the hearts of men (and women). And if it addresses many of the problems that plague all peoples who attempt to live together in societies, it does so on the terms of those who were able to cast the auto-biography of the male individual as the collective history of humanity. The old truths about the importance of history still obtain: history *does* constitute a kind of collective memory and memory *does* provide the only foundation for identity, informed choice, and, yes, freedom. Our age has proved itself uneasy with history, has permitted itself to wonder whether history still has a bearing. Perhaps things have changed so much and so fast that the wisdom of the past is dead—or merely no longer relevant.

History is not the main problem, however out of fashion its virtues may be. We know—and here I am speaking as a historian and a woman—however little we like to acknowledge, that the individual and collective life of peoples inescapably throws up the intractable problems of mortality, morality, and politics. No, the problem lies in the relation between history and auto-biography. For a long time, many of us had accepted the constraint of interpreting our personal stories through the prism of an official story, and official standards of excellence. We did so because we accepted the story as objective. In recent decades, two things have changed. First, we have been encouraged to place a greater premium on our personal story than that of anyone else, however prestigious. Second, we have learned that most stories that purport to be objective are in fact someone else's story.

We can no longer restore the original version of the Great Tradition as everybody's autobiography. We know that it was not. Nor can we afford to surrender to the anarchy of an infinite number of personal autobiographies. Our Great Tradition has a different purpose: It constitutes the collective history without which none of our individual stories makes sense. We now face the challenge of rewriting it as a collective history that is not the monopoly of a single group, a single perspective. The orphans of the Great Tradition must reclaim it for themselves, for only they, and those who accept their just claims, can revitalize it for us all.

Suggestions for Further Reading

DWIGHT ST. JOHN

Daniel Boorstin, having published *The Discoverers* (New York, 1983), is at work on a companion volume. In the present essay he esteems the humanistic scholar as a "courier of time" to an age inclined to dismiss the past. This theme implies a regret over the triumph of science and the ubiquity of electronic media. Boorstin nevertheless recommends *The Voice of the Dolphins* (New York, 1961), science fiction by the great physicist Leo Szilard. The impact of new information technologies on scholarship and on a culture's sense of time is argued in two still provocative books by Marshall McLuhan, *The Gutenberg Galaxy* (Toronto, 1962) and *Understanding Media: The Extensions of Man* (New York, 1964). Ernest Gellner's work returns insistently to what he calls "the great divide": the profound dislocation that occurs when a pre-scientific culture becomes a scientific culture, one whose epistemological norms are drawn increasingly from scientific philosophy and practice. His book *Thought and Change* (Chicago, 1965) has sobering implications for humanists. Boorstin's title recalls Emerson's 1837 oration "The American Scholar," included in the attractive new Library of America volume of Emerson's *Essays and Lectures*, edited by Joel

Porte (New York, 1983). For T. S. Eliot's "Tradition and the Individual Talent," see *The Sacred Wood* (London, 1920).

Richard Maxwell Brown supplied copious notes to his essay "Violence in American History," including his *Strain of Violence: Historical Studies of American Violence and Vigilantism* (New York, 1975). A thorough study of the Second Amendment is Carl Bakal's *The Right to Bear Arms* (New York, 1966). Frank Norris's *The Octopus* is available in paper from Signet.

Leon Cooper's fluid style and humane learning can be seen in his textbook *An Introduction to the Meaning and Structure of Physics* (New York, 1968). Among recent writings on creationism, see the series of essays by Stephen Gould in *Hen's Teeth and Horse's Toes* (New York, 1983) and *Scientists Confront Creationism* (New York, 1983), edited by Laurie Godfrey. Gould's *Ever Since Darwin: Reflections on Natural History* (New York, 1977) is accessible to the layman. The thirty-five-year reign of quackery in Soviet genetics and, indeed, in all the sciences that affect agriculture is the subject of David Joravsky's detailed *The Lysenko Affair* (Cambridge, Mass., 1970). On Galileo, see Giorgio de Santillana's *The Crime of Galileo* (Chicago, 1955). Ernest Gellner's *Thought and Change* treats the "contemporary discomfort" felt by people whose traditional understanding of what it means to be human (free will, dignity) has been undermined by scientific knowledge and, more subtly, by the very methodology of science itself. On metaphor outside a purely aesthetic context, see *Metaphor and Thought*, edited by Andrew Ortony (New York, 1979),

W. H. Leatherdale's *The Role of Analogy, Model, and Metaphor in Science* (New York, 1974), and Robin Lakoff's *Metaphors We Live By* (Chicago, 1980). Stephen Pepper's *World Hypotheses* (Berkeley, 1942) shows that many important philosophical systems are based on metaphors (e.g. the world or nation-state as a mechanism or an organism). See also Thomas Kuhn's influential *The Structure of Scientific Revolutions* (Chicago, 1962). Theodore Roszak's characterization of the scientist as Frankenstein (cited by Cooper) may be found in "The Monster and the Titan: Science, Knowledge, and Gnosis," *Daedalus*, vol. 103, no. 3 (Summer 1974), pp. 17–32.

Jaroslav Pelikan's latest statement on the humanities, "Humanism—Two Definitions and Two Defenses," appears in *Southern Humanities Review*, vol. XIX, no. 3 (Summer 1985). His most recent book is *The Vindication of Tradition* (New Haven, 1984), a product of the 1983 Jefferson Lectures in the Humanities. Readers interested in Emerson will enjoy Gay Wilson Allen's biography *Waldo Emerson* (New York, 1981). Other valuable studies include Sherman Paul's *Emerson's Angle of Vision* (Cambridge, Mass., 1952); Stephen Whicher's *Freedom and Fate: An Inner Life of Ralph Waldo Emerson in His Time* (New York, 1979); and David Robinson's *Apostle of Culture: Emerson as Preacher and Lecturer* (Philadelphia, 1982). Emerson is at the heart of F. O. Matthiessen's *American Renaissance: Art and Expression in the Age of Emerson and Whitman* (London, 1941).

In recent years, James Cox has published notable essays on two American autobiographies: "Jefferson's *Autobiography:* Recovering Literature's Lost Ground"

(*Southern Review*, XIV [October 1978], pp. 633–52) and "Learning Through Ignorance: *The Education of Henry Adams*" (*Sewanee Review*, LXXXVIII [Spring 1980], pp.198–227). William McFeely's *Grant: A Biography* (New York, 1981) is now the standard life. The nature of biography, and especially autobiography, has been richly explored in the last ten years or so, as increasingly sophisticated methods of analysis have been developed. An ideal place to begin is James Cox's "Autobiography and America" in *Aspects of Narrative*, edited by J. H. Miller (New York, 1971, pp. 143–72). Cox develops a definition of autobiography and shows why it is an important genre in our national literature. Another American student of autobiography, James Olney, has written *Metaphors of Self: The Meaning of Autobiography* (Princeton, 1972) and has edited *Autobiography: Essays Theoretical and Critical* (Princeton, 1980). See also William Spengemann's *The Forms of Autobiography* (New Haven, 1980), which includes a long bibliographic essay on the study of autobiography. Ira Nadel's challenging new book, *Biography: Fiction, Fact, and Form* (New York, 1984), argues that a biography is inescapably fictive: its subject's lived reality is inaccessible, and from the fragments of his life the biographer must construct—not merely discern—a coherent story. A fascinating recent experiment in autobiography is *Roland Barthes by Roland Barthes* (New York, 1977). Chronology is abandoned and we are offered, instead, an alphabetically arranged list of topics. The epigraph reads: "It must all be considered as if spoken by a character in a novel."

If biographers tend to resemble either novelists or historians, the historians themselves, according to

William McFeely, must recapture a working space between the imaginative blandishments of the novelists and the arid quantifications of the social scientists. Perhaps the most famous and controversial recent text of the "Cliometricians" is Robert Fogel and Stanley Engermann's *Time on the Cross* (Boston, 1974), a study of the slave economy in the United States. Herbert Gutman's rebuttal, *Slavery and the Numbers Game*, appeared almost immediately (Urbana, 1975). Historical novels, such as Gore Vidal's *Lincoln: A Novel* (New York, 1984), have long crowded the bestseller lists. Even the blurring of the boundary between history and fiction, as in E. L. Doctorow's *Ragtime* (New York, 1975), has many precedents. Truman Capote's *In Cold Blood* (New York, 1966) and other recent self-conscious attempts to write a "nonfiction novel" are examined in John Hollowell's *Fact and Fiction: The New Journalism and the Nonfiction Novel* (Chapel Hill, 1977). Hayden White's *Metahistory: The Historical Imagination in Nineteenth Century Europe* (Baltimore, 1973) seeks to identify and study the various paradigms—each based on a particular poetic trope, such as metaphor or irony—which underlie the texts of several great historians and which determine what is to count as a "historical explanation." It is a difficult but important book.

Hayden White would no doubt concur with Elizabeth Fox-Genovese that "no story is either innocent or transcendent." What would history look like if seen through the eyes of women? And how should teachers of history take account of those substantially excluded from the "story"? In her essay in the present volume, Fox-Genovese describes her project for the Organization of American Historians, *Restoring Women to History*. See also Gerda Lerner, *The Majority Finds Its Past* (New York, 1979) and *Liberating Women's History: Theoretical and Critical Essays*, edited by Berenice Carroll (Urbana, 1976). Barbara Haber's *Women in America: A Guide to Books, 1963–1975* (Urbana, 1981) provides unusually full annotations; an appendix covers books published from 1976 to 1979. Elizabeth Janeway's most recent books are *Powers of the Weak* (New York, 1980) and *Cross Sections from a Decade of Change* (New York, 1982). The full text of William Bennett's NEH report on undergraduate education, "To Reclaim a Legacy," appears in *The Chronicle of Higher Education*, November 28, 1984. Elizabeth Fox-Genovese has also written *The Origins of Physiocracy: Economic Revolution and Social Order in Eighteenth-Century France* (Ithaca, 1976) and, with Eugene Genovese, *The Fruits of Merchant Capital: Slavery and Bourgeois Property in the Rise and Expansion of Capitalism* (New York, 1983).

Contributors

Daniel J. Boorstin, Librarian of Congress since 1975, is one of the nation's foremost social and intellectual historians. Among his many books, his principal work is *The Americans*, published over a fifteen-year period, with the last volume, *The Democratic Experience*, being awarded a Pulitzer Prize in 1974. Dr. Boorstin's latest work is *The Discoverers* (1983), and he is currently at work on a companion volume.

Richard M. Brown has published extensively on the subject of his essay in this volume, his principal work being *Historical Studies of American Violence and Vigilantism* (1975). He is currently Beekman Professor of Northwest and Pacific History at the University of Oregon.

Leon Cooper won the Nobel Prize in Physics in 1972; his publications on his scientific research and on the place of science in the modern world have been widely recognized. At Brown University he holds the positions of Watson Professor of Science and co-director of the Center for Neural Science.

James M. Cox, a member of the faculty at Dartmouth College for many years, has written a variety of books and essays on such subjects as Henry James, Hawthorne, Poe, Frost, Emerson, and, especially, Mark

Twain and American humor. His most recent scholarship has addressed the genre of autobiography.

Elizabeth Fox-Genovese has combined a scholarly interest in traditional fields of history (*The Origins of Physiocracy*, 1976; and, with Eugene Genovese, *The Fruits of Merchant Capital*, 1983) with that of the movement to coordinate women's history into "mainstream" history. Generally regarded as the leading theoretician of this latter activity, she is a member of the faculty at the State University of New York, Binghamton.

Taylor Littleton is general editor of the multi-volume Franklin Lectures series and has edited other works on Elizabethan literature and the history of drama. Following a ten-year period of service as academic vice-president at Auburn University, he was in 1983 appointed Mosley Professor of Science and Humanities.

William S. McFeely has taught at Yale and the University of London, and is presently Mellon Professor of the Humanities at Mt. Holyoke College. He has published widely in the area of Civil War history, with his *Grant: A Biography* winning a Pulitzer Prize in 1981.

Jaroslav Pelikan's works on Martin Luther and St. Augustine, and his multi-volume *The Christian Tradition* have made him one of the world's leading theological historians. Sterling Professor of History at Yale since 1972, he was chosen by NEH in 1983 to deliver the annual Thomas Jefferson Lecture, which was published in 1984 as *The Vindication of Tradition*.

Dwight St. John is assistant professor of English at Auburn University and is a member of the scholarly team at work on the variorum edition of Robert Browning. In 1985–86 he is serving as visiting professor of English language and literature at Hunan University in China.

Index

Cold Harbor, battle of, 6, 128, 129, 130
Coleridge, Samuel Taylor, 50
Common law, 103
Confederate Army: battle of Gauley Bridge, 126
Connelly, Thomas L., 162
Conway, Moncure, 69
Cooper, Leon, 1, 2, 3, 4, 7, 12
Corday, Charlotte, 207
Corinth, battle of, 6
Cox, James M., 1, 5, 10, 162
Crabbe, George, 23
Crane, Stephen, 172, 173, 174, 176, 178
Creationism: view of, 87, 88, 89, 90, 91, 92, 93, 94
Creationists, 7
Creon, 204
Crockett almanacs, 19

Dana, Charles A., 133
Dante, 84, 86, 87, 89
Danton, George Jacques, 207
Darwin, Charles, 8, 38, 80, 87
Darwinism, 11
Dew, Thomas Roderick, 188
Dioscorides, 25
Doctorow, E. L., 169
Donelson, battle of, 129, 156, 157, 158
Doré, Gustave, 84; illustration of Satan, 85
Dowdey, Clifford, 126

Early, Jubal, 142
Edison, Thomas, 30
Edwards, Jonathan, 20
Einstein, Albert, 81, 84
Eisenhower, Dwight D., 137, 196
Eliot, T. S., 31
Elizabeth I, 194, 198, 204
Emerson, Charles, 36

Emerson, Edward Waldo, 54
Emerson, Ralph Waldo, 1, 3, 4, 5, 8, 9, 12, 15, 16, 35–75 passim; *Nature*, 4, 36–67 passim; *Representative Men*, 4, 36, 54–72 passim; *Journal*, 35, 40–66 passim; Natural History Society lectures, 37; resignation from pastorate of Second Church in Boston, 37, 61; essays and lectures on astronomy, 42, 43; κόσμος or beauty, 44, 45, 48, 49; Divinity School Address, 61, 62; view of caste, 63, 64, 65; view of fate, 64, 65; view of man's moral nature, 65, 66, 67, 68, 69
Emerson, William, 36, 37, 68
English Civil War: women of, 206
Enobarbus, 13
Evolution: theory of, 90, 91, 92. *See also* Darwin, Charles
Experimental Researches in Electricity (Faraday), 39

Faraday, Michael, 39
Faulkner, William, 126
Fermi, Enrico, 30
Fifth Monarchy: radicals of, 206
Foote, Shelby: narrative of Civil War, 128, 142
Ford, Henry, 21, 22
Fox, George, 58
Fox-Genovese, Elizabeth, 2, 4, 5, 10
Frankenstein, The Modern Prometheus (Mary Shelley), 78
Frankenstein monster: images of in relation to science, 78, 79
Franklin, Benjamin, 134, 136, 147
Franklin Lectures Series: purpose of, 1, 12; subject matter of, 35
Freeman, Douglas Southall, 126, 142

French Revolution: history of, 195, 208; women of, 206, 207
Freud, Sigmund, 80

Gable, Clark, 166
Galen, 25
Galileo, 81, 82, 83
Gettysburg: Pickett's charge at, 129
Girondins, 207
Goethe, 48, 57, 59, 68, 69, 70, 71, 72
Gone With the Wind (Mitchell), 165–66
Gouges, Olympe de, 207
Grand Army of the Republic: reunion of, 138
Grant, Ulysses S.: as general, 1, 5–6, 8, 9, 125–59 passim, 162, 166, 167, 168, 176, 177, 178, 179; as president, 6, 8, 9, 10, 131, 147; as writer, 128, 131, 135–59 passim
Gunn, Jacob, 168

Halleck, Henry, 154, 155, 156; orders from Grant, 157, 158
Hamlet, 13–14
Hayes, Rutherford B., 8
Henel, Heinrich, 71
Herodotus, 33
Heroes and Hero Worship (Carlyle), 59
Hines, Thomas S., 182, 183
Historian: difficulties of, 19; role of, 22
Hobbes, Thomas S., 181
Holmes, Oliver Wendell, 54
Homer, Winslow, 133
Homestead Ethic, 98–101, 109, 117, 118; defined by Brown, 6; viewed by rural Americans, 7, 10
Hood, John B., 142

Hooker, Joseph, 130, 174, 175, 178, 179
Howard, O. O., 178
Howells, William D., 138
Humanists: claims of, 30
Hume, David, 80

Ibarruri, Delores, 204
Industrial Revolution. *See* Republic of Letters
Intruder in the Dust (Faulkner), 126–27
Iuka, battle of, 141

Jackson, Thomas J. (Stonewall), 179
Jacobins, 207
Janeway, Elizabeth, 203
Jenner, Edward, 42
Joan of Arc, 198
Johnson, Andrew, 174–75
Johnston, Albert Sidney, 141
Johnston, Joseph E., 126, 129
Johnston, Mary, 126
Johnston, William Preston, 156

Kant, Immanuel, 31
"Killed at Resaca" (Bierce), 178

Lee, Robert E., 126, 128, 129, 130, 131, 133, 137, 142, 146, 152, 153, 154, 158, 175, 179; unconditional surrender of, 130
Leeuwenhoek, Anton van, 26
Leibnitz, Baron Gottfried Wilhelm von, 26
Levellers, the, 206
Leviathan (Hobbes): quotation from, 181
Libraries: types of, 28
Library of Congress, 27, 28
Lincoln, Abraham, 128, 129, 131, 134, 158, 167, 168, 174, 175, 196

Roszak, Theodore, 78, 94
Rousseau, Jean Jacques, 212
Royal Society in London, 26, 29
Science: effects of, 25, 76–96;
    dominance of, 27; rise of, 25–
    26, 31; role of, 11. *See also*
    Technology
Scoresby, William, 47
Scott, Winfield, 154
Selden, George, 22
Shakespeare, William, 13, 14, 31,
    59, 67, 70–71, 188, 190, 204
Shelley, Mary, 78, 79
Sheridan, Philip, 142, 157
Sherman, William T., 142, 155
Shiloh, battle of, 6, 10, 128, 129,
    141, 148, 151, 156
Shylock, 190
Smith, Adam, 95
Smith, Henry Nash, 58
Snow, C. P., 35
Sophocles, 204
Southern Honor (Wyatt-Brown),
    169
Southern Pacific Railroad: effect on
    settlers, 6
Spanish-American War, 173
Spotsylvania, battle of, 128, 130,
    156
Stanford, Leland, 10
Stegner, Page, 50
Stein, Gertrude, 133, 146
Swayne, Wager, 178
Swedenborg, Emanuel, 59, 63, 66
Szilard, Leo, 17, 30

Taylor, Zachary, 154
Technology: application of, 1;
    compared to science, 3–4; histo-
    ry of, 21–22; republic of, 1, 11,
    13, 23. *See also* Science
Thomas, Emory, 162

Thomas, George H., 142
Thucydides, 165
Toynbee, Arnold J., 194
Truman, Harry S., 137, 196
Twain, Mark, 6, 138, 139, 140,
    143, 150, 177
"Two Cultures": theme of, 35

Unconditional surrender, of Lee,
    130

Vicksburg, battle of, 128, 140, 152
"Voice of the Dolphins, The"
    (Szilard), 17

Warren, Robert Penn, 12, 76, 96,
    177
Washington, George: Marshall's bi-
    ography of, 19
Washington College: Lee as presi-
    dent of, 131
Watson, James, 29
Waud, Alfred, 133
Webster Publishing Company, 140
Weisskopf, Victor, 79
When the War is Over (Becker),
    174–75, 179
Whitman, Walt, 136
Whittier affair, 139
Wilderness, battle of the, 128, 129,
    141, 151
Wilhelm Meister (Goethe), 68
Williams, K. P., 142
Wilson, Edmund, 177
"Women of Ideas and What Men
    Have Done to Them": title, 202
Woodward, C. Vann, 176
Wordsworth, William, 50
Wyatt-Brown, Bertram, 169, 181

Young Emerson Speaks (McGiffert),
    37
Young Frankenstein (Brooks), 78